TIMELESS BIOGRAPHIES

# A Star Named Bibha and Other Stories

**Anwesha Sengupta**  **Supurna Banerjee**  **Simantini Mukhopadhyay**

*Illustrated by*
Mistunee Chowdhury

HarperCollins *Children's Books*

First published in India in 2024 by HarperCollins *Children's Books*
An imprint of HarperCollins *Publishers*
Building No. 10, Tower A, 4th Floor, DLF Cyber City,
Phase II, Gurugram, 122002, India
www.harpercollins.co.in

2 4 6 8 10 9 7 5 3 1

Text © Supurna Banerjee, Simantini Mukhopadhyay and Anwesha Sengupta 2024
Illustrations © HarperCollins *Publishers* India 2024

P-ISBN: 978-93-5699-449-2
E-ISBN: 978-93-5699-446-1

Supurna Banerjee, Simantini Mukhopadhyay and Anwesha Sengupta assert the moral right to be identified as the authors of this work.

While every effort has been made to ensure the accuracy of the facts presented in the book, the publishers are not in any way liable for any errors that might have crept in.

The views and opinions expressed in this book are the authors' own and the facts are as reported by them. The publishers are not in any way liable for the same.

All rights reserved. No part of this publication may be reproduced, stored in a retrieval system, or transmitted, in any form or by any means, electronic, mechanical, photocopying, recording or otherwise, without the prior permission of the publishers.

Cover and inside illustrations by
Mistunee Chowdhury

Typeset in Sabon 13.5 pt/19.5 pt
by Veena, Bookwatch

Printed and bound at
Nutech Print Services - India

This book is printed on FSC® certified paper which ensures responsible forest management.

# CONTENTS

*Authors' Note* .................................................. 5

1. Fatima Sheikh ............................................. 7
2. Swarnakumari Devi ..................................... 13
3. Pandita Ramabai Saraswati .......................... 19
4. Miss Asho .................................................. 25
5. Bhikaji Cama .............................................. 31
6. Sushila Sundari .......................................... 37
7. Durgabai Kamat ......................................... 43
8. Rokeya Sakhawat Hossain ........................... 49
9. Muthulakshmi Reddy .................................. 55
10. Amrit Kaur ................................................. 63
11. Jaddanbai .................................................. 69
12. Ammu Swaminathan .................................. 75
13. Parbatibai Bhore ........................................ 81
14. Chandraprabha Saikiani .............................. 87
15. Helen Lepcha ............................................. 93

16. Bibha Chowdhuri .................................................. 99

17. Sarala Thakral .................................................. 105

18. A. Lalitha .................................................. 111

19. Chakali Ilamma .................................................. 117

20. Amrita Pritam .................................................. 123

21. Vidya Munshi .................................................. 129

22. Sulagitti Narasamma .................................................. 135

23. Urmila Eulie Chowdhury .................................................. 141

24. Meera Mukherjee .................................................. 147

25. Shantabai Kamble .................................................. 153

26. Fatima Beevi .................................................. 159

27. Mary D'Souza Sequeira .................................................. 165

28. Arati Saha .................................................. 171

29. Tun Tun .................................................. 177

30. Sudesha Devi .................................................. 183

    *Glossary* .................................................. 190

    *Famous Personalities* .................................................. 193

    *List of Sources* .................................................. 198

# Authors' Note

Who were the women achievers of nineteenth and twentieth century India? How did caste, class, religion and physical ability shape their journeys? In this book, we write about thirty such exceptional women. These were women who, through their lives and work, challenged the norms of the time. They challenged what women could and could not do. From a scientist to a labourer, a farmer to a comedian, a school teacher to an engineer, a film star to a writer – the book accommodates women from various walks of life to show how they pushed boundaries and worked to make the world a more equal space.

In this book, we celebrate the diversity of these women's experiences, keeping in mind the times they lived in and the ways in which their identities shaped their experiences and opportunities. We hope the lives of these women will inspire and empower young readers to understand the past and the contemporary with empathy.

– Anwesha, Simantini and Supurna

# FATIMA SHEIKH
## Lighting Up Lives

Most nineteenth-century parents did not send their daughters to school. The few who did were criticized by others. Girls had to fight for their education. One of the earliest turfs of this struggle was Poona in the 1800s. Foremost among the warriors for girls' education was Fatima Sheikh. She is regarded as one of the first female educators of India. Fatima's life is entwined with that of Savitribai Phule, the first Indian woman to become a teacher and start a school for girls. While we celebrate and honour the life of Savitribai, Fatima remains forgotten.

The dates of Fatima's birth and death are uncertain. Some say that she was born on 9 January. Not much is known about her early life either. She knew how to read and write from an early age, which was very unusual for girls at that time. Her brother, Usman, encouraged her to do a teacher-training course. Fatima met Savitribai when they were enrolled in a teacher-training institution run by an American missionary, Cynthia Farrar. They graduated together and became lifelong friends.

Savitribai Phule and Fatima Sheikh, as well as Savitribai's husband, Jyotirao Phule, understood the need to educate girls. They also realized the importance of educating Dalits. Hindu society is divided into several groups, called castes. In the nineteenth century, caste was very important among traditional and conservative Hindus; it determined what one could eat, where they could go, whom they could marry, what occupation they could pursue and with whom they could share a meal. Dalits were believed to be at the very bottom of the caste pyramid. As a result, they were poor, mostly illiterate and severely oppressed by members of the higher castes.

When Jyotirao and Savitribai expressed a desire to help educate women and Dalits, Jyotirao's father threw them out of his house. Fatima and Usman provided refuge to the couple in their home. This home went on to become the first girls' school in the country in 1848. Running this school was a daunting task; the society at the time was against the idea of girls going to school, and even more so against girls of all religions and castes studying together under one roof. Fatima's act therefore was one of great love and courage. The Muslim clergy did not appreciate her efforts to introduce modern education to Muslim girls. They claimed that educating girls went against Islam. Fatima argued that Islam did not prohibit girls' education.

Fatima managed and taught in the school that she helped set up along with Savitribai. Initially, there was very little enrollment in the school, as parents were not willing to send their daughters out of the house to get an education. Fatima went from door to door, counselling parents about the importance of school learning. Both Savitribai and Fatima faced violent opposition from upper-caste men and women in their quest. They threw stones and cow dung at the two women. They were threatened with physical harm. Fatima was called names and subjected to harsh treatment by the Muslim community. But Fatima's fight continued. Slowly, girls from different castes, economic backgrounds and religions started coming to the school. In a community where girls from different families did not mix socially, the school brought them under the same roof. Later, Jyotirao Phule established two trusts, the Native Female School, Poona, and the Society for Promoting the Education of Mahars-Mangs. These were initially looked after by Savitribai and then Fatima.

The history of Indian education speaks glowingly of many great educators, such as Ishwar Chandra Vidyasagar, Swami Dayananda and Mahadeo Govind Ranade, who made modern education possible for different sections of people. Most of these are men belonging to the upper castes. Little is written about women like Fatima Sheikh. Savitribai and Jyotirao Phule spoke of her with great respect and fondness. As a Muslim woman fighting for a casteless society and modern education for girls, Fatima Sheikh is an inspiration for future generations of educated young girls to assert themselves.

# SWARNAKUMARI DEVI

## The Tagore Girl
## Who Wrote About Women

Swarnakumari Devi was the fourth daughter of Debendranath Tagore, a renowned philosopher and religious reformer. Though the Tagores were highly educated and had a forward-thinking approach, following the customs of the day, they did not send their girls to school. The Tagore girls were married off at an early age. Unlike most families of those days, however, erudite tutors visited the Tagore home to teach their daughters and daughters-in-law. There were no restrictions on what girls could read.

Swarnakumari was an avid reader. At a very young age, she started writing poems and stories. Her elder brothers, Jyotirindranath and Satyendranath, encouraged her. The Tagore household was a hub of creativity. The brothers and sisters wrote plays and acted in them. Some of them were painters, and some others were music composers and singers. Over the years, several of the Tagore siblings served as editors of the popular Bengali literary magazine *Bharati*. Swarnakumari would go on to serve as the editor of *Bharati* for eleven years.

When she was thirteen, Swarnakumari was married off to Janakinath Ghoshal, who belonged to a traditional Hindu family. Her husband's family disowned him when he adopted Brahmoism, a reformed version of Hinduism. Swarnakumari became a mother when she was just fourteen. After that, she gave birth to three more children. She was only twenty-five when her youngest daughter, Urmila, died. Her daughters Hiranmoyee and Sarala grew up to become educationists and social workers.

Janakinath was a kind and industrious man. He became a successful businessman and later was one of the founders of the Indian National Congress. He appreciated Swarnakumari's talents and encouraged her. When she was twenty, Swarnakumari wrote a historical novel called *Deepnirvan*. Over a period of fifty years, she wrote numerous short stories, poems, plays, songs, novels, charades, serious articles and travelogues. Her books were widely read in Bengal, and the English translation of her novel *Kahake* was a bestseller in England. During her tenure as the editor of Bharati, she wrote many articles on women's issues. Swarnakumari herself was interested in history, geography, science and anthropology. Apart from fiction, she wrote lucid essays on complex subjects for the readers of *Bharati*.

While upper-caste men enjoyed many privileges, the women in their families had to obey a number of oppressive religious rules and customs. They suffered a lot in the name of tradition and rituals. These women did not have the right to own property or the right to work. Since they could not leave their husband's home, they were burdened with housework and childcare and oppressed in several other ways.

Famous and talented male authors of her time, however, often glorified these practices. Bankimchandra Chattopadhyay, for instance, wrote that pious women in ancient India willingly jumped into the pyres of their husbands when they became widows. Swarnakumari's writing offered a different take on these practices. It showed that though upper-caste women rarely protested against these oppressive practices, their silence could not be seen as consent.

In Swarnakumari's time, widow remarriage was unacceptable in upper-caste society. Yet, men were allowed to have more than one wife. Swarnakumari strongly condemned the practice of polygamy and the discrimination against widows. In her short story *Amarguchchha,* a young widow touchingly expresses her desire to feel loved and wanted. Swarnakumari chose friendship and sisterhood among women as a dominant theme in her stories. In her story *Lajjabati,* a young, coy and nervous bride finds a confidante in her married sister-in-law. In her humorous pieces, Swarnakumari often mocked upper-caste men who displayed their knowledge in front of their wives, who were not allowed to study.

Swarnakumari was associated with the Indian National Congress. She established an organization named Sakhi Samiti that worked for the welfare of widows and orphans. In Bengali, 'sakhi' means a female friend. The organization educated widows, who were later employed to teach other women.

Swarnakumari was fortunate to be born in the Tagore family since it exposed her to the writings of world thinkers. However, she was often denied recognition within her family. Her younger brother, the world-famous poet Rabindranath Tagore, believed that Swarnakumari's ambition surpassed her talent. He disapproved of Swarnakumari's works, saying that they lacked originality since she had little knowledge of the outside world. The outside world, however, saw her differently. She was immensely popular as a writer and her books were bestsellers. An author, a poet, a playwright, a composer, a columnist, an editor, an educationist and a reformer, Swarnakumari Devi was an exemplary woman who wore many hats.

# PANDITA RAMABAI SARASWATI

## The Scholar-Reformer

In 1858, amidst the forests of Gungamul in the Western Ghats, Ramabai was born to a Marathi family. Her father, Ananta Dongre, was a Sanskrit scholar. In those days, women and Dalits were not allowed to learn Sanskrit. But Ananta wanted to teach his wife Laxmibai this language. When his relatives and neighbours opposed the idea, Ananta left home and settled in the forest. There he introduced Laxmibai to Sanskrit. Their youngest daughter was Rama. Little Rama also learnt Sanskrit from both her parents. And she was very good at it.

In 1876, a famine spread across southern and south-western India. Millions of people had nothing to eat. Ananta, who was old and had lost his eyesight by then, died in the famine. So did Laxmibai. Rama and her elder brother survived. Together they travelled to various parts of India, reciting Sanskrit scriptures at various gatherings. Finally, they reached Calcutta. The learned men of the city soon heard about Rama's excellent command over Sanskrit and the scriptures. They called her to test her skills. Rama impressed them so much that she received two titles – Pandita and Saraswati. Pandita means an expert, and Saraswati is the Hindu goddess of learning. Rama was the first woman to receive these honours.

In Calcutta, Rama got married to Bepin Behari Madhvi. Theirs was an exceptional match for many reasons. High-caste girls were generally married off between the ages of eight and twelve at that time. Rama was twenty when she became a wife. Girls did not choose their own husbands, but Rama did. More importantly, she married a person who belonged to a caste different from hers, something that was not encouraged in Hinduism. But Rama and Bepin went ahead and had a non-religious marriage. Though Ramabai was an expert of Hinduism, she did not practise every aspect of it.

Unfortunately, Bepin died within two years of the marriage. After his death, Rama moved to Poona with her infant daughter. At this time, many brave individuals were fighting for the rights of women in Maharashtra. This might have attracted Rama to Poona. Here, she set up the Arya Mahila Samaj to educate women and to spread awareness about the evils of child marriage.

India had very few women medical practitioners at that time. Conservative Indian families did not allow women to be treated by male doctors. Therefore, women often did not get any treatment when they were ill. This inspired Ramabai to become a doctor. In 1883, Ramabai left for England to study medicine. To fund her travel, she wrote a book called *Stree Dharma Neeti*, in which she referenced Hindu mythology to explain the need for women's education. Very few women at that time could think of raising money from writing to fund their travels. They could travel only with the support of their fathers and husbands. Rama had neither. Rama needed neither.

English medical schools, however, refused to admit Ramabai. They found her to be physically unfit for the profession. Doctors discovered that Rama had a hearing impairment. Instead of supporting her, the schools chose to keep her out. But Rama did not give up. She learnt English, mathematics and the natural sciences. She studied Christianity and became a follower of that faith.

Rama was friendly with some of the other courageous Indian women of her time. Anandibai Joshi, a Marathi like her, was one of them. Anandi also wanted to become a doctor. She went to the United States to study medicine. When Anandibai's education was complete, Rama sailed to the United States from England to witness her graduation ceremony.

Ramabai loved America. There, girls went to school and took up careers. Ramabai was impressed to see disabled people using technology for a better life. Being deaf herself and the daughter of a blind father, she had deep empathy for disabled people. After returning to

India in 1889, she built a shelter home for young widows and orphans, where all the residents received education. Rama introduced special techniques to teach blind students in this home. She wrote a book called *Hindu Upper Caste Women* to raise the initial money for her work. This was a remarkable book that highlighted the oppressive customs and practices that upper-caste women were forced to follow.

Over the years, Ramabai's shelter home, Mukti Mission, expanded to include hundreds of widows, orphan children and children rescued from epidemics and famines. Mukti Mission still exists with branches across India, making the lives of thousands of women and children better. In them Ramabai lives on.

# MISS ASHO

## And Then There Was Light

When Swarna was growing up in Calcutta and Rama was learning Sanskrit amidst the woods of the Western Ghats, far away from them, in the historic city of Lahore, lived a little girl named Aysha. Aysha had a rather sad childhood. In 1864, when she was three years old, she had smallpox. At that time, smallpox was a deadly disease which killed many every year. Though she recovered from smallpox, she lost her eyesight as a result of the disease, a very common side effect. Little Aysha could no longer see anything or anyone.

From the 1850s, a few British men and women had become involved in teaching children in northern India. They opened schools and hostels in Lahore, Amritsar and Ludhiana. In many of these schools, blind children were welcomed. In Lahore, Emma Fuller and Mary Fuller took the initiative. The two sisters opened seventeen schools in and around Lahore for children. Aysha's parents admitted her to one of these schools when she turned ten. Her teacher was Miss Emma. Though she did not know the specific technology used to teach words and letters to children who could not see, she was determined to help Aysha in every possible way. Emma thought of interesting and novel methods to teach her stories and songs from the Bible and subjects like geography and general knowledge.

When Aysha was fourteen years old, tragedy struck again. Her parents died and she became an orphan. Her elder brother wanted her to get married immediately. Perhaps he thought this would give her some security and stability in life. He found a blind maulavi (Muslim religious preacher) of Lahore for Aysha. But Aysha was not ready for marriage. She wanted to study further. When she could not convince her brother, she went to her teacher, Miss Emma, for help. Emma gave her a home to stay in temporarily. Thus began the next chapter of Aysha's life.

Emma, her sister and other British women who were involved in teaching students like Aysha had deep faith in Christianity. They were missionaries who taught their students the stories and philosophies of Jesus Christ and the Christian faith. Some of them encouraged the students to become followers of Christianity. Aysha, a Muslim by birth, became Miss Asho, a Christian, under the influence of Emma.

After Aysha became Asho, she was sent to a boarding school in Ludhiana to study before she could become a teacher herself. In 1886, Asho began teaching the blind women of Amritsar. She remained a dedicated teacher for forty years. A blind Englishman called William Moon had developed a form of type in the 1840s to help visually impaired people read with the help of their fingers. It came to be known as Moon Type. Asho learnt Moon Type and taught it to others. She was, perhaps, the first Indian woman to become a teacher trained in special techniques for the visually impaired. She also learnt and taught to knit and visited a local hospital to recite from the Bible. But, like her mentor Emma Fuller, Asho tried to convince her students, their families and others to convert to Christianity. Forcing someone to convert to another faith is based on the false notion that one religion is better than another. Perhaps because Christian women had helped Asho in difficult times and because she had studied the Bible since childhood, she started believing in the superiority of the religion.

In 1911, the British government counted fourteen blind people in every ten thousand Indians. This was a huge number. But the government did little to meet their needs, educate them or employ them. They built a few eye hospitals in big cities like Calcutta (now Kolkata), Bombay (now Mumbai) and Madras (now Chennai) and a few shelter homes across the country. But the government paid no attention to the education of the blind children of the country. The missionaries taught the children to read, write and recite. The children learnt to make mats, sew and knit. Aysha or Asho was one of those who devoted her life to making the lives of others a little better. Though the missionaries believed in the superiority of the Christian faith, like Asho, they helped others and spread love, not hate.

# BHIKAJI CAMA
## The Lady With the Flag

In August 1907, several politicians from across the world gathered in the German town of Stuttgart. They believed that every country should be free of foreign domination, and that land and other properties should be collectively owned by people and not by some individuals. They wanted to make policies that would end poverty and treat everyone as equals. There was an Indian woman among them. When she stood up to speak, she hoisted a tri-coloured flag and declared: 'Behold, the flag of independent India is born! ... In the name of this flag, I appeal to lovers of freedom all over the world to support this [Indian freedom] struggle.' Everyone was surprised. India, at that time, was ruled by the British, and the Union Jack was considered the Indian flag. But this woman refused to accept the Union Jack. She had designed a flag for her country and wanted everyone at the meeting to show their respect to it. This woman was Bhikaji Cama. History remembers her as the first person to hoist an Indian flag in a foreign land.

Bhikaji was born in a Parsi merchant family of Bombay in 1861. The Parsis of Bombay, like the Brahmos of Calcutta, were progressive people. Parsi women attended schools, travelled alone in carriages and some even managed businesses. Bhikaji went to an English-medium school and became interested in the politics of the country. From a young age, Bhikaji supported the Indian freedom movement against the British. She firmly believed that India should be governed by Indians and not by white men from a distant country. But she was married to a man who did not share her love for the country. Rustomji Cama, her husband, had great admiration for British culture and wanted British rule to continue. Bhikaji, however, did not agree with him and continued to support the freedom movement. This was extraordinary, as women of that time, even the most elite of them, were expected to obey their husbands.

In 1896, Bombay was badly hit by a plague epidemic. Hundreds and hundreds of people had died. Bhikaji volunteered at Grant Medical College and took care of the plague victims as much as she could. But, soon, she herself caught the disease. Though she recovered, she remained weak for a few years. In 1902, on a doctor's recommendation, she travelled to England for faster recovery. But the trip extended beyond what she had initially planned.

In England, she met Dadabhai Naoroji, a fellow Parsi who was famous for his criticism of British economic policies. He, along with Lala Hardayal and Shyamji Krishna, was also working for India's freedom movement from abroad. Bhikaji started working with them. The

British government did not like her activities. They said if she wanted to return to India, she would have to stay away from the freedom movement. Bhikaji did not agree to this condition. As a result, the British rulers did not allow her to return to her own country. Living in exile was a matter of great sorrow for her. It was only in 1935, when she was on her deathbed, that Bhikaji was allowed to come back to India.

During her time away from India, Bhikaji travelled to several countries in Europe and Africa, where she remained politically active. Along with other freedom fighters in exile, she published and distributed texts criticizing British rule, attended political conferences and meetings to make people aware about the British oppression in India and raised funds to support those who were fighting the British at home.

Bhikaji dreamt of an India and of a world where men and women were equal, people of all religions were equal, and everyone was free. In a political meeting in Egypt in 1910, she asked everyone: 'Where is the other half of Egypt? I see only men, who represent half the country! Where are the mothers? Where are the sisters? You must not forget that the hands that rock cradles also build persons.' Similarly, she wanted more Indian women to participate in the fight for their country's freedom. She spoke in support of women's right to vote.

The flag that Bhikaji unfurled in Germany had some similarities with today's national flag. It had three colours: green, saffron and red. Green symbolized the Muslims, saffron the Hindus and red all the other religions of India. The flag also had eight lotuses, perhaps because British India had eight provinces. Vande Mataram, a popular nationalist slogan, was written on the middle strip, and on the lower section were the sun and the crescent moon, again symbolizing Hindus and Muslims. Thus, Bhikaji's India recognized and celebrated many religions. Now it is our task to keep India as Bhikaji wanted it to be – a land for all, irrespective of gender and religion.

# SUSHILA SUNDARI

## The Woman Who Tamed the Tigers

Circuses are great fun! Have you ever seen one? In the olden days, there would be clowns, magicians, trapeze artists and colourfully dressed women and men performing tricks with animals. Many moons ago, when there were no televisions, computers, video games or amusement parks, the circus was the most popular medium of entertainment for children and even adults.

In the late nineteenth century, a circus came to India from Europe. Two famous circus groups—Wilson's Great World Circus and Chiarini's Great Italian Circus—toured the country in the 1870s. They became very popular. There was a big crowd to watch them wherever they went. Inspired by them, Vishnupat Chatre started the Great Indian Circus in 1880 in Maharashtra. This was the first Indian circus. In Bengal the first circus, called the Great Bengal Circus, was established by Priyanath Bose in 1887. In this circus, there were some very brave and famous performers. One of them was a woman named Sushila Sundari (Sushila the beautiful). She was the first Indian woman to perform in a circus.

Born in 1879 in northern Calcutta, Sushila was a remarkably talented woman. From childhood, she was very good at physical exercises. In the circus, she could showcase her skills and earn money. Kumudini, her sister, also joined the Great Bengal Circus. Kumudini became well known for her performance with horses. But more than Kumudini, the audience appreciated Sushila.

At the Great Bengal Circus, under the guidance of Priyanath Bose, Sushila became a great gymnast and trapeze artist. She could ride a horse as well. But Sushila was best known for two events. One was where she would be buried alive for more than ten minutes under four feet of sand. After ten minutes, she would come out alive and fresh. Anyone else would have died of suffocation. But Sushila had mastered the art of breath control. The other event was perhaps even more daring. The Great Bengal Circus had two tigers, gifted by the king of Rewa, a small princely state in Central India. After the tigers came to the circus, the Great Bengal Circus became even more famous and started making more money. So the people at the circus named them Laxmi and Narayan after the Hindu deities of prosperity. Sushila tamed Lakshmi and Narayan. Once the tigers became familiar with her, she started performing with them on stage. Sushila would enter the cage of Lakshmi and Narayan fearlessly and play with them. Whoever saw Sushila perform was struck by her courage. In those days, the British often portrayed Bengalis as cowards. Bengali women were considered timid and, barring a few elite girls, they mostly stayed at home. Sushila showed the world that given a chance, a sari-clad Bengali woman could even tame a tiger! Unfortunately, it was because of a tiger that Sushila's career came to a stop. Once when Sushila was performing with a tiger called Fortune, she was severely injured. Fortune was new at the circus and did not know Sushila well. Perhaps Fortune was afraid of Sushila and attacked her in self-defence. After this incident, Sushila had to retire from the circus. The accident taught Sushila and others that being careful was as important as being courageous.

For Sushila, the Great Bengal Circus was her home. Priyanath Bose was like a father to her. She made friends and fell in love with a magician in the circus. She inspired other women as well to join the circus. Apart from her own sister, the Great Bengal Circus had another woman performer named Mrinmoyee. In the early twentieth century, these women broke the usual stereotype of Bengali women being shy, timid, obedient and homebound. Many Bengalis saw Sushila as an example of their community's courage and power. Soon Bengal would witness a widespread anti-British movement known as the Swadeshi Movement, where the Bengalis would boycott British products, celebrate the beauty of their land and their own bravery and courage.

At a time like this, Sushila and her friends in the Great Bengal Circus became symbols of Bengali power.

Today the circus is no longer as popular as it used to be. There are cartoons and video games to entertain children. Moreover, the government has banned the use of almost all animals in the circus as they are often ill-treated by the circus management. Nonetheless, if a circus comes to your town, do pay a visit and remember Sushila Sundari, the woman who could tame tigers!

# DURGABAI KAMAT
## Setting Off to the Film Set

Little Durga was hardworking, talented and pretty. She was a curious child with many interests. Her father was a renowned musician. When she was a child, Durga learnt to play musical instruments such as the veena, tabla and sitar. She could sing, dance and paint. Durga belonged to a Marathi Brahmin family which, like most upper-caste families of that time, was very conservative. In her community, girls received little education and were married off early. They were not supposed to have a career. After Durga completed Class 7 in school, her father found a match for her.

The groom was a Marathi Brahmin named Anand Nanoskar. Soon after her marriage, Durgabai realized that Nanoskar was an abusive husband. Their daughter Kamlabai was born in the year 1900. Nanoskar neglected his family and did not do his duty towards Durgabai and Kamla.

Durga was an exceptionally strong and brave woman. She did not want to stay in the marriage. But, regardless of the torture she faced, breaking a marriage was unthinkable for a woman of her social status. Even today, many women are compelled to stay in abusive and unhappy marriages because of the difficulties of living alone. Things were much harder then. How would she raise her daughter? Where would she live? What would she do for a living?

One option for Durga was to work as a domestic help in other people's houses. Another was to use her talent and skill in singing and dancing to become a theatre actor. Acting in the theatre was not considered a respectable profession in those days, more so for upper-caste women. Durgabai chose to break the taboo. Holding the hand of three-year-old Kamla, she left her home to join a theatre company. Her family members tried to dissuade her. When they could not, they severed all ties with her. The only person who supported her was another strong woman, her mother-in-law. She offered Durga jewellery and a house that she could sell and use the money to start her life afresh as an independent single mother.

It was not easy to find a job at a theatre company. In those days, men played the roles of women. Durga's talent made them insecure, and some of them even threatened to quit their jobs if Durga was employed alongside them. They feared that women like her would take their jobs away. This hostility did not dampen Durgabai's spirits. She found a job at a theatre house called Chittakarshak Natak Company. She and Kamla travelled with the company. While she would play the leading female roles, Kamla would act as a child artist. They staged Indian mythological stories and Marathi translations of Shakespeare's plays. The audience loved the performance of the mother-daughter duo. Kamla could not attend regular school because of the travelling. Durgabai arranged for her to be educated at home. 'Home', however, was not a fixed place for Durga and Kamla. Once they had staged a few shows in one place, the theatre company would move to a neighbouring village. A few days ahead of the move, the manager of the theatre company would rent a large hall, where the team would stay.

Life had many surprises in store for these two amazing women. There was a man called Dhundiraj Govindrao Phalke, popularly known as Dadasaheb Phalke, who had directed India's first full-length feature film, *Raja Harishchandra*. He had not been able to find a woman to act as Raja Harishchandra's wife, Taramati. A man named Anna Salunke had played the role. When Kamla was thirteen, Phalke approached the manager of Chittakarshak Natak Company for his second film, *Mohini Bhasmasura*. It was a silent film. He wanted to cast Durgabai in the role of Goddess Parvati and Kamla as Parvati's daughter, Mohini. The manager agreed and history was made. Durgabai and Kamlabai became the first Indian female actors cast in a film. Even after this, many people considered it improper for women to act in films. Men continued to take on female roles for many years.

Little is known about the rest of Durga's life. As she grew old, she saw her daughter become a strong woman like her. Kamlabai too acted in theatre and films. She raised her children single-handedly after her husband died at a very young age. With time, Indian cinema emerged as a field where women would make very significant contributions. Sadly, the mother-daughter pair that set the stage for such progress remains largely forgotten.

# ROKEYA SAKHAWAT HOSSAIN

## The Begum and Her Dreams

Have you heard of Ladyland? It is a wonderful world where there are no mosquitoes, no epidemics, no pollution, no dirt. There is soft, green grass and beautiful flowers everywhere. Just like Barbie Land, Ladyland is run by women – all highly educated and hardworking. They use sunlight for cooking and they know how to control rainfall. They have even invented cars that fly! Everyone in this wonderland loves and respects everyone else. The men in Ladyland stay inside the house, take care of babies and do all the domestic work.

More than a century ago, Rokeya, a girl from Bengal, visited Ladyland in her dreams. She was married to a busy bureaucrat named Khan Bahadur Sakhawat Hossain. Mr Hossain would often travel for work. Sitting alone in her home, Rokeya imagined a different world – a world where men would stay at home and women would do all the outside work. One day, she wrote a story about this imaginary Ladyland and named it 'Sultana's Dream'. It was published in 1905 in an English periodical. It was an extraordinary story. Living in a time when women were hardly allowed to come out of their homes, Rokeya imagined a world where women were free, highly educated and more powerful and efficient than men. Rokeya could think of such a world because she knew that there was nothing that women could not do. She was a feminist. In other words, she believed that men and women were equals.

Born in 1880 in a village named Pairaband in eastern Bengal, Rokeya, like most girls of her time, never went to school. She learnt to read and write Bengali and English at home. Her elder brother, Abu Ali Saber, and sister, Karimunnesa, were her teachers. At the age of eighteen, Rokeya was married off to Sakhawat Hossain, an Urdu-speaking bureaucrat. Sakhawat admired Rokeya's interest in education. He encouraged her to read and write, particularly in Bengali. This was exceptional. Elite Muslims, including Rokeya's own father, looked down on the Bengali language and believed Arabic and Persian were a mark of scholarship. But Sakhawat, an Urduwallah, did not have any such objection.

Apart from 'Sultana's Dream', Rokeya wrote many essays, short stories, poems, novels and satirical pieces. In these writings, she repeatedly mentioned the poor condition of women in Indian society, the abuse they suffered and the unfair norms and traditions they had to follow. Rokeya also wrote about the need for educating Muslim girls. Most of her writings were in Bengali and they were published in famous periodicals like *Saogat, Mohammadia, Mahila* and *Naoroz*. Rokeya became a famous writer and thinker of her time.

Rokeya, however, wanted to be more than a writer. She was a passionate supporter of women's education and wanted to educate as many girls as she could. To this end, Rokeya started a girls' school after Sakhawat's death in 1911. She named the school after him – Sakhawat Memorial Girls' School. The school was established in Bhagalpur, Bihar, where her husband had some property. After a few months, Rokeya moved to Calcutta and with her moved her school.

In Calcutta, there were a few girls' schools at that time. Christian missionaries had started building schools for girls from the second half of the eighteenth century. In these schools, girls were taught to read, write and do needlework. But these schools were only for Christians. In 1849, John Elliot Drinkwater Bethune, a lawyer by profession and an educator by passion, opened a school in Calcutta that welcomed girls from all religions. Following him, some Hindu and Brahmo men became interested in education for girls. A few more girls' schools were established across Bengal. Muslims, however, stayed away from school education. Some families, like that of Rokeya's, preferred to teach their girls at home. Others did not think educating women was important. In this context, Rokeya's Sakhawat Memorial Girls' School became very important. She personally approached various Muslim families and requested them to send their girls to her school. Initially, very few responded positively. In Calcutta, Sakhawat Memorial began with nine students and two benches! Gradually though, more and more students joined the institution. Over the years, it became one of the best schools in the city. Even today, the West Bengal government runs the school.

Rokeya died in Sodepur near Calcutta in 1932. But her life and writings have inspired generations of women and men to dream and work towards a more equal world.

# MUTHULAKSHMI REDDY

## The Doctor Who Made a Difference

In 1886, a little girl was born in Madras Presidency. When she grew up, she changed the lives of many. This little girl was Muthulakshmi Reddy. Muthulakshmi was born to Narayanswamy, principal of a college, and Chandramal, a Devadasi. Devadasis were women from the so-called low castes who were supposed to be given in marriage to the Hindu gods. They were considered to be of low social status because of their caste and job. So, when Muthulakshmi's father, a Brahmin, decided to marry a Devadasi, his family was very angry and cut off all ties with him.

Belonging to the Devadasi tradition and being close to her maternal family, Muthulakshmi faced many difficulties in childhood. When she went to school, boys ran behind her bullock cart, mocking her for going to school. Only three of the forty students in Muthulakshmi's class were girls. In the classroom, the boys and girls were separated by a screen. Despite the fame and glory of erudite women like Swarnakumari, Ramabai, Bhikaji and Rokeya, many parents were hesitant to send their daughters to school. Muthulakshmi was particularly disliked by the parents of the other students because she was the daughter of a Devadasi. They feared she would corrupt the other children.

But Muthulakshmi was determined. With the help of her father's training, she passed matriculation and excelled. She became the first woman to be admitted to Maharaja's College, which had been a men's college till then. Muthulakshmi made more history when she enrolled herself in a medical college in 1907, becoming the first woman to do so. She chose surgery as her specialization. Her teachers discouraged her. They felt that surgery was not for the faint-hearted and that as a woman, she would not be able to handle the sight of blood. But Muthulakshmi again proved everyone wrong. She scored hundred per cent in her surgery examination. She went on to become the first woman House Surgeon in the Government Maternity and Ophthalmic Hospital in Madras.

When her younger sister died of cancer, a heartbroken Muthulakshmi decided to specialize in cancer treatment. She went to London to learn more about the disease and its treatment. She returned from London to set up the Adyar Cancer Institute in Madras. Much later, under the Women's Indian Association, she started the Cancer Relief Fund.

Muthulakshmi was remarkable not only as a student and a doctor, she was a reformer too. She had seen the misery that her cousins and others faced because of the stigma of the Devadasi system. She was determined to fight this. From an early age, she was influenced by the teachings of Mahatma Gandhi and Annie Besant. She even gave up an active medical practice to dedicate her time to the public service of women and children. She became one of the earliest members of the Women's Indian Association, which was founded in 1927 to support women. Realizing the importance of political power to make positive changes, she went on to become the first Indian woman legislator as a member of the Madras Legislative Council. In this role, she took many initiatives to end the dismal conditions of women, especially poor women of low-caste families. She proposed a law against dedicating young girls as Devadasis to Hindu temples. She also fought to ban the practice of hiring Dalit women to breastfeed babies born in wealthy families. This was a common practice which was not fair to Dalit mothers and their children. They had to deprive their own babies of nutrition to feed other babies. Muthulakshmi objected to this injustice. She joined activists like Sister Subbalakshmi in a fight for widow remarriage and education. This was a time when girls were married off at a very young age. Muthulakshmi fought to raise the age of marriage for girls to sixteen. As a fierce believer in women's rights, she, like Bhikaji Cama, also advocated for voting rights for women.

As a young girl, Muthulakshmi had seen the difficulties faced by girls of backward castes, and lack of any support structure for them. Young girls who wanted to escape the Devadasi system had no place to go. Women's hostels were ruled by caste laws, and lower-caste girls were not allowed there. To provide refuge for them, she started Avvai Home in Madras in 1931. This was a place for young girls to stay, and provided them training in nursing, teaching, carpentry, handicraft and home science. Her vision was to equip these girls to get jobs and earn for themselves. Later she set up a separate hostel for Muslim girls. She provided scholarships to the Harijan Girls' Institute so that little girls from Dalit families could study.

Muthulakshmi faced opposition for breaking established social laws. Powerful men, like Congress leader C. Rajagopalachari, opposed her fight to end the Devadasi system. After a long fight of seventeen years, the law was finally passed. She also brought the Anti-Polygamy bill, which stopped men from marrying more than once. While Muthulakshmi had opponents, she also had strong supporters, like her husband Dr Sundara Reddy. Theirs was a marriage of love, respect and equality.

# MUTHULAKSHMI REDDY

Muthulakshmi Reddy achieved much. She spent her life trying to make the lives of others around her better. Her life teaches us how to be brave, compassionate and determined.

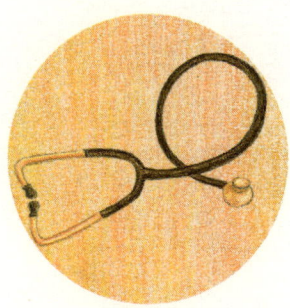

# AMRIT KAUR

## The Princess With a Purpose

On 2 February 1889, a baby girl was born to the royal family of Kapurthala, a small kingdom surrounded by the state of Punjab. Her parents named her Amrit. To the rest of the world, she would be known as Rajkumari Amrit Kaur – a freedom fighter, a close aide to Mahatma Gandhi, a women's rights activist and a cabinet minister in independent India.

Born with a silver spoon in her mouth, Amrit grew up in luxury and went to England for her education. When Amrit returned to India in 1918, the royal life did not interest her anymore. Around this time, the freedom struggle against British rule was gaining strength in India. It caught the attention of the princess. Like the Parsi nationalist Bhikaji Cama, this girl from Punjab was also eager to free her motherland from foreign rule. Amrit's father, Raja Harnam Singh, was a good friend of the famous Congress leader, Gopal Krishna Gokhale. Gokhale had a great influence on young Amrit. Her interest in the freedom struggle and her anger towards the British further grew when the Jallianwala Bagh shooting happened. On a day in the April of 1919, a crowd had gathered at Jallianwala Bagh, near Amritsar, to peacefully protest against the arrests of some Indian freedom fighters. Dyer, a British brigadier-general, ordered to shoot at the protesters without any reason. At least a thousand people died that day. This incident disturbed Amrit very much. Around this time, she met Mahatma Gandhi and was mesmerized by his philosophy and simplicity. Amrit later worked as Gandhi's secretary for sixteen long years, leaving her luxurious life behind. As she bravely participated in the fight against the British, she was sent to prison several times. But the fearless princess of Kapurthala never quit the battleground.

Apart from fighting the British, Amrit was enthusiastic about women's causes. She was a strong critic of the purdah system, which was practised by different communities in India. Like Muthulakshmi, she repeatedly spoke against the custom of child marriage and the Devadasi system. As a founder member of the All India Women's Conference, Amrit strongly promoted women's education.

After India became independent, Amrit Kaur became the first health minister of the country. Diseases like malaria, tuberculosis, cholera and smallpox were widespread at that time. As a health minister, she spent time and energy in educating people about the symptoms and treatments of malaria. Because of her efforts, as the years passed, fewer and fewer people died of this disease. Amrit also encouraged Indians to take the vaccine for tuberculosis. As health minister, Amrit moved away from Gandhi's teachings. Gandhi did not always have faith in western medicine. He often depended on natural and herbal therapies if he was unwell. But the princess did not share Gandhi's beliefs on medical science. This proved that Amrit, though a great admirer of Gandhi, did not always follow him. She had a mind of her own and did what she thought was right.

During her years as health minister, Amrit played a leading role in establishing the All India Institute of Medical Sciences (AIIMS) in New Delhi. Even today, AIIMS is one of the best government hospitals and a premier medical college of India. People, both rich and poor, come to AIIMS from across the country for treatment and education. Amrit also knew that India urgently needed good nurses. In 1950, when she was the health minister, there was only one trained nurse for every 43,000 Indians. This was not enough, and many had to depend on untrained domestic workers or family members for taking care of the sick. Unknowingly, the untrained caregivers sometimes gave wrong medicines. They could not always identify symptoms of diseases, and the patients would suffer. So, Amrit encouraged the young girls of the country to take up nursing as a profession. She also wanted Indian girls to become doctors and teachers.

The princess was known for her love for sports as well. A fantastic tennis player herself, she had won many tournaments in her youth. As health minister, she continuously spoke of the physical benefits of sports. At her insistence, the Government of India sanctioned grants from 1953 for sports coaching. This became known as the Rajkumari Amrit Kaur Coaching Scheme and covered sports like hockey, tennis, table tennis, cricket and athletics.

Amrit, the patriotic princess, worked for an India where all women and men would be equal, and they would be healthy, happy and free. Unlike the princesses of fairy tales, Amrit did not wait for a prince to come and marry her. Rather, she led India from the front. Now it is for us to ensure that India remains a country where freedom and equality are celebrated, and a healthy life is within the reach of common people.

# JADDANBAI

## The One-Woman Show

In the beautiful city of Bombay, there once lived a remarkable woman called Bai Jaddanbai. She wrote poems, set them to music and sang them delightfully for Hindi films. That made her a lyricist, composer and singer – all in one. She and Saraswati Devi were the earliest female composers in the Indian film industry. Jaddanbai also had her own company that produced movies. She played the leading role in these movies. Some of these movies, like *Madam Fashion,* were also directed by her. Bai Jaddanbai was thus a film director, an actress and a film producer as well. There were only two women film directors at that time – Jaddanbai and Fatima Begum. Jaddanbai excelled in everything she did. Her films were superhits. If the radio did not play her songs, people wrote angry letters to the newspapers. In her time, there was no one like her in India. Bai Jaddanbai was a phenomenon.

Born in Allahabad in 1892, Bai Jaddanbai had a very talented mother. Her name was Dilipa Devi. Dilipa Devi had a lovely voice and could dance very gracefully. But in those days, girls from respectable Hindu families were not allowed to sing or dance in public. Dilipa left home and joined a group of performers. She converted to Islam, named herself Daleepbai and married a sarangi player, Miyajaan. Jaddanbai was their daughter. From her childhood, Jaddanbai was trained as a classical singer. When she was five years old, her family shifted to Calcutta, where she spent the next thirty-five years. Here, she learnt music from famous classical singers like Shrimat Ganpat Rao, Ustad Moinuddin Khan, Ustad Chandu Khan Saheb and Ustad Laab Khan Saheb. After learning from them and practising regularly, Jaddanbai became famous. The rajas of various states invited her to their court to listen to her ghazals and thumris. She also started singing for the radio.

In 1931, when Jaddanbai was thirty-nine years old, the first Indian talkie *Alam Ara* was made. Till then, Indian movies did not have any soundtrack. But now that sound was added to films, Jaddanbai started receiving film offers. Her film career started in the city of Lahore, which is now in Pakistan. After acting and singing in a few films, she decided to move to Bombay and open her own company. Her company, Sangeet Studio, produced several films, including *Talash-e-Huq* (1935), *Madam Fashion* (1936), *Hriday Manthan* (1936), *Moti Ka Haar* (1937) and *Jeevan Swapna* (1937). These films were very popular. Everyone loved the music and Jaddanbai's acting. After watching *Talash-e-Huq,* a journalist described her as 'the golden voiced star'. *Madam Fashion* was praised as a 'fine musical extravaganza'. Her daughter Nargis also had small roles in some of these films. Later, Nargis became a famous actress.

Nargis's father was Mohandas Uttamchand Tyagi. Jaddanbai called him Mohanbabu. Mohanbabu did not work. Jaddanbai earned enough to run the family. At that time, women generally stayed at home and their husbands earned a living. This made Jaddanbai and Mohanbabu different from others. Jaddanbai made a lot of money as she had very good business sense. She bought an expensive limousine for her family.

Mohanbabu was a Punjabi Hindu who became a Muslim after marrying Jaddanbai. But in their family, no one was fully Hindu or fully Muslim. Jaddanbai sometimes called herself Jayadevi and practised many Hindu rituals. She gave her daughter Nargis a Hindu name—Tejeswari—as a second name. Like her mother, Nargis also married a Punjabi Hindu, Sunil Dutt. In their family, religion never came in the way of love.

Jaddanbai had a strong and courageous personality. In her Calcutta house, she apparently had a pet tiger. Her neighbours called her Garjanbai (garjan is the Bengali word for roar). She was respected by all in the Bombay film industry. Whenever there was any quarrel in the film industry, Jaddanbai was called to settle it. She had another talent. She could learn languages very easily and was fluent in Urdu, Arabic, Persian, Bengali and Hindi. She loved to read, drive, swim and play tennis.

After Jaddanbai's death in 1949, Nargis gifted her Calcutta house to the government to build a training centre for disabled people.

Today we see many talented women in every Indian film. They act, sing, produce, direct and edit films, and operate the camera. They are here because once there were women like Jaddanbai.

# AMMU SWAMINATHAN

## The Social Crusader

Have you ever heard of a book called the *Constitution of India*? It is the book of laws and principles that every Indian has to follow. It was prepared by a committee of three hundred and eighty-nine people, headed by the great Dr B.R. Ambedkar, who fought for the improvement of Dalit communities. Fifteen of the committee members were women. One of these women was Ammu Swaminathan. Ammu was born to Govinda Menon and Anakkara Vadakath Ammuamma in 1894 in Palakkad district of Kerala. She was their youngest child. She lost her father very early. Her mother took care of her and her siblings and managed the house amidst difficulties. Being brought up by such a strong woman shaped Ammu's personality and thoughts.

At the age of thirteen, following the trend of the time, Ammu was married off to Subramma Swaminathan. She was twenty years younger than Subramma. When Subramma asked her if she would marry him, Ammu laid down her conditions for the marriage. At that time, rarely did women have a say in their marriages. But this teenager made it clear that this was not to be the case for her. She wanted to move to Madras and master the English language. This was also a time when women's movements outside the house were strictly monitored by the family. But spirited Ammu was not having any of that. She told Subramma that, just like no one asked her brothers what time they would come back home, she should also never be asked that question. Subramma agreed to all the conditions laid down by her. They got married in 1907. Ammu belonged to a caste lower than that of her husband. So Subramma's family boycotted the ceremony and did not accept the marriage. The Nair community that Ammu belonged to had a system of marriage called 'Sambandam', which allowed women to take more than one husband. In this community, children could not inherit their father's property. Both Ammu and Subramma rejected this practice and got their marriage registered in England instead. Ammu and Subramma had a happy marriage based on love and respect. Subramma encouraged Ammu to develop her talents.

Ammu, like Muthulakshmi and Amrit, was a follower of Gandhi and decided to participate in the national freedom movement. Her social and political work began in 1914. In 1917, she founded the Madras branch of the Women's India Association (WIA). WIA was one of the first associations to demand women's right to vote and equal rights for them in general. Ammu was thus a feminist. Years later, in 1934, when she joined the Indian National Congress, she continued her fight both for her country and for the women of the country. She actively participated in the great Quit India Movement in 1942. Led by Gandhi, it demanded the end of British rule in India. Ammu was jailed for participating in this movement.

Ammu Swaminathan was a crusader against caste inequalities as well. While in jail, she heard an upper-caste woman derogatorily calling out to a lower-caste woman as 'sudrachi' (a woman of low caste). She walked up to that woman and told her that she, Ammu, was a 'sudrachi' too, referring to her Nair identity.

In 1945, Ammu was elected as a part of the Provisional Parliament of India from Madras and went on to become one of the members of the committee set up to draft the constitution of independent India. She was proud of the spirit of the constitution and the equal representation provided to men and women in its making. At the same time, practical-minded Ammu criticized it for its length. She was elected a member of the Lok Sabha in 1950 and served till 1957. Then she was nominated as a member of Rajya Sabha from 1957 to 1960. She also served as a goodwill ambassador to various countries. As someone who faced child marriage, she fought against it in the parliament. As a member of the Lok Sabha, she pushed for maternity benefits for working women.

Ammu and her husband had four children: two daughters and two sons. Both her daughters became famous in their own right. Captain Lakshmi Sahgal, the leader of the Rani Jhansi regiment of the Indian National Army, was her second born. Her youngest daughter, Mrinalini Sarabhai, became a very famous dancer. Ammu Swaminathan lost her husband in her thirties. As a young woman, she refused to follow regressive widowhood practices, such as shaving the head and wearing a white sari. Her personal and professional life contains many lessons for us. At a time when India is facing many crises, we should revisit her address to the Constituent Assembly: 'I think if we are to deserve this Constitution we have to make up our minds to work it into something alive and something that will be of benefit to every citizen of this country. I know that the Constitution gives us in the Fundamental Rights, equal status, adult franchise […] but […] we have to see that these ideas and ideals which are on paper in the Constitution are implemented by the people of this country.'

# PARBATIBAI BHORE

## The Workers' Warrior

Being a working woman in this country has always been difficult. Women in the labour force are sometimes paid less than men. They have to balance their work with their housework, and quite often their jobs are considered less valuable than men's. Like today, this injustice was not accepted by workers in the past either. Many joined workers' organizations called trade unions to fight for their rights. Parbatibai Bhore was one such woman.

Parbatibai was born in Bombay to a barber's family in the early 1900s. They were extremely poor and lived in a chawl. Their next-door neighbour was the famous Dr B.R. Ambedkar. Young Ambedkar was already an erudite man. In her autobiography *An Account of One Brave Woman* (which she dictated), Parbati recalls how they could only see books inside his room. Inspired by this, Parbati and her father were eager for her to go to school and learn. But her mother was reluctant as she feared that poor and low-caste girls were treated badly at school. Decades had passed since Savitribai Phule, Jyotirao Phule and Fatima Sheikh had started their schools to teach Dalit children and others who were less privileged. Many schools, however, were yet to welcome Dalit pupils, and upper-caste parents did not want Dalit classmates for their children. Despite these problems,

Parbati's father supported her wish to study and sent her to school.

At the age of nine, Parbati was married to a person who worked at her father's barber shop. Parbati did not have a happy married life. Her husband quarrelled with her and called her names. Parbati was not a stranger to violence. Her father was supportive of her education. But he was a violent man who beat his wife. Her husband's house felt like a prison to her. After twelve years of marriage, Parbati peacefully protested against the violence and injustice and tried to live life on her own terms within the marriage.

Parbati started as a worker in a textile mill in Bombay in 1928–29. This was a period of workers' movements in Bombay's textile mills. Under the leadership of the communists, over two lakh workers joined a strike to demand better work conditions. B.T. Ranadive, S.A. Dange and other important trade union leaders organized classes to teach the workers about labour laws and their rights. By participating in the strike and attending these classes, Parbati came to understand the way in which workers could assert their rights if they came together. Once again, in 1939, workers went on strike against the unjust mill owners. Half the women workers in the mills were suddenly sacked by the owners.

The other workers did not come to work to protest against the layoffs. Parbati was an active participant in this strike. In 1940, there was another general strike by workers of all the mills in Bombay for better and fairer working conditions. Workers were made to toil hard under difficult conditions with very little compensation. They wanted better wages, bonus and fair price shops to buy things at a cheaper rate. But the owners were not willing to listen to the workers' demands. With cooperation from the government, they arrested the main leaders behind the protest – Ranadive, Dange and others. At this point, Parbati came forward and took over the leadership of the movement. In 1941, she became the secretary of Girni Kamgar Union, an important trade union of textile mills. She fought injustice not just in her home but also in the workplace. For her growing popularity and leadership role, she was arrested by the Maharashtra government.

Parbati's responsibilities as a leader did not remain restricted to Bombay. She travelled to other parts of India, like Kanpur, to give speeches. Her speeches were very popular and encouraged others to speak up for their rights. She was even invited to speak in other countries like Austria and Denmark. But the government did not give her permission. Parbati's fame and popularity made many men in the Communist Party and trade unions jealous. They did not want her to lead movements. They were used to women in subordinate roles, not as leaders. Many of them started spreading ugly rumours about her. But none of this stopped Parbati from pursuing her course.

Parbati showed what courage and determination meant. Her autobiography is aptly titled *An Account of One Brave Woman*. In the male-dominated society that she lived in, she had to fight at every level. She fought violence in her own home, fought injustice against herself and other workers in the workplace and also fought the government that arrested her. Even today movements and strikes do not always recognize women as leaders and activists. But women like Parbatibai Bhore showed the important role women can play in protecting their rights as women and as workers.

# CHANDRAPRABHA SAIKIANI

## Fighting for Freedom

It was 1914. A girl who had just stepped into her teens motivated a group of young girls to assemble together to form an informal school in a remote village in Assam. She wanted to teach them everything she'd learnt in the boys' school that she'd attended till then. She and her sister, Rajaniprabha, would walk through a long, muddy path every day to school since there weren't any girls' schools close to her house. Named Chandrapriya Mazumdar by her parents Ratiram and Gangapriya Mazumdar, she chose the name Chandraprabha Saikiani for herself. The seventh of eleven children, Chandraprabha grew up to be a strong-willed woman, who made path-breaking choices throughout her life.

Impressed with their interest in education, a school sub-inspector, Neelkanta Barua, awarded Chandraprabha and Rajaniprabha scholarships to attend the Nagaon Mission School. Soon after they joined the school, they came to know that only Christian girls were allowed to stay in the hostel. Chandraprabha was enraged by such discrimination and protested to the authorities. Her efforts were successful, and soon girls from different backgrounds were admitted to the school's hostel. She could not tolerate discrimination and oppression. A few years later, she protested when she found out that the so-called low castes were forbidden to enter a Hindu temple in Assam. Those days, many temples across India did not allow certain castes or women to enter their premises. Chandraprabha's movement opened the doors of the temple to everyone, irrespective of caste or gender. At a time when few women entered the public space, Chandraprabha excelled in public speaking from a very young age. She fought relentlessly for women's right to education and work and was the pioneer of the women's rights movement in Assam. Like Chandraprabha, Rajaniprabha too loved studying, and grew up to become the first woman doctor in Assam.

Chandraprabha was a rebel. When her parents arranged her marriage with a much older man, she protested. She fell in love with her friend, an Assamese writer called Dandinath Kalita. Dandinath was creative, but traditional and meek. He loved Chandraprabha, but he knew that his family would not approve of their marriage, since they belonged to different castes. They were happy together for some time and had a son. However, Dandinath followed his family's orders and married a younger girl from his caste. Heartbroken, Chandraprabha accepted the separation with courage and dignity. She raised her son, Atul, as a single mother in a society that was not at all friendly to women, especially to single mothers.

Chandraprabha's childhood dream was realized when she became the headmistress of a girls' school in Tezpur. She worked with progressive Assamese leaders like Omeo Kumar Das and Chandranath Sharma. She worked at a number of schools and quit her job when the authorities started interfering with her political involvement. Chandraprabha joined the Non-Cooperation Movement (1920–22) led by M.K. Gandhi and inspired many women to do the same. While fighting for the country's freedom, she took up the cause of oppression of women.

In 1925, she attended a session on the importance of education organized by Assam Sahitya Sabha, a literary organization. She was irked by the seating arrangement at the ceremony. The men sat in the front rows while the women were made to sit behind a barrier made of bamboo. She asked the women, 'How can there be equal opportunities if women are made to sit in the back, separated from the men?' The women were quick to respond. They broke the barrier and came to the front to sit with the men. She had exceptional courage to break the norms and inspired other women to do so.

Chandraprabha worked as the editor of *Abhijatri*, the mouthpiece of Assam Pradeshik Mahila Samiti, the women's rights organization that she founded and led.

She wrote a number of books in Assamese. Some of her works include *Pitribhitha, Sipahi Bidrohat* and *Dillir Sinhasan*. She was jailed twice for her participation in India's freedom struggle. In 1957, she contested the Assam Legislative Assembly elections but was defeated.

Chandraprabha suffered from cancer towards the end of her life and died on her seventy-second birthday. Just before her death, she received the Padma Shri from the Government of India. Today there are many educational institutions in Assam named after her. Based on her life, Assamese litterateur Nirupama Borgohain wrote a novel called *Abhiyatri: One Life Many Rivers*. Though she is remembered fondly today, during her lifetime, Chandraprabha received little recognition for her indomitable courage. Her struggles, however, influenced the lives of many women of her time.

# HELEN LEPCHA
## Coding in the Dough

Many years ago, the great freedom fighter Subhas Chandra Bose was under house arrest in the hill town of Kurseong. He was forbidden by the British police to speak to anyone except the domestic workers. Nobody, except a handful of his spirited aides, knew that he was planning to escape from Kurseong to Calcutta and then to Kabul. Among these aides was Helen Lepcha, lovingly called Helen Didi by the people of Kurseong. She helped Bose plan his escape. Helen's husband, Ishan Ahmed, ran a bakery, which supplied the bread for Bose's breakfast. Helen wrote secret messages in the bread and Bose replied in the same way. Finally, Bose, disguised as a Pathan, escaped from Kurseong to Calcutta. It was later known that the dress he wore during his escape was designed and made by Helen.

Helen was a remarkable girl. Born to Mr and Mrs Achung Lepcha in a remote hilly village called Sangmu in the southern part of Sikkim, Helen had six siblings. After her birth, the family moved to Kurseong, a beautiful town surrounded by mountains. It had good schools and provided ample opportunities for work. Helen went to school till she was fifteen. In her growing years, Helen witnessed the struggle for independence from British rule. She heard the speeches of important leaders who came from Calcutta to the hills. One such speech motivated Helen so much that she joined the freedom struggle when she was still a teenager. In 1918, she went to Calcutta, where her sister lived. There she learnt how to spin the charkha. She excelled at it and was selected to represent Calcutta at the Khadi and Charkha Exhibition organized in Bihar.

Bihar had witnessed a devastating flood in 1920. Helen visited the flood-hit areas and was moved by the suffering of the people. Thousands of people had lost their homes and had nothing to eat. Helen worked tirelessly to provide relief to the people of Bihar. M.K. Gandhi, who had come to visit the flood-affected people, met Helen and was very impressed with her selfless service. He invited her to his ashram at Sabarmati in Gujarat. Helen accepted his invitation, and a new chapter of her life started.

Gandhi gave Helen a new name – Sabitri Devi. She became an active member of the labour union of the Congress party and a leader of the labourers' movement in Bihar and Uttar Pradesh. The labourers in the coal fields in these areas mostly came from tribal backgrounds and were severely exploited by the British managers. They worked in inhuman conditions and could be sacked any moment at the whims of the manager. The workers loved and respected her. In 1921, as a part of Gandhi's

Non-Cooperation Movement, Helen held the tricolour and led a procession of 1,000 workers from the coal fields of Jharia in Bihar. The British became wary of her rising popularity among the workers and issued a warrant against her. She fled to escape arrest and finally took shelter in Jawaharlal Nehru's house in Allahabad. There she met important leaders of the Congress party. However, when the Non-Cooperation Movement was at its peak, Helen's mother fell ill. Helen had to return to Kurseong to look after her ailing mother.

By then, the freedom movement had spread to the hills. The workers in the tea plantations were angry because they did not have even the most basic facilities at work. Like the coal mine workers, they too found a leader in Helen Didi. Helen organized a team of local youth and visited the houses of the residents, asking them to boycott foreign goods and to use the charkha. At the same time, women leaders like Sarala Devi, daughter of Swarnakumari Devi, Maniben Patel and Basanti Devi were promoting the charkha in other parts of India. Like them, Helen too was arrested by the British police. After spending three months in jail, she had to stay under house arrest for a period of three years till 1925. The people of Kurseong loved her dearly, and she became the first elected woman commissioner of Kurseong Municipality in 1936.

Helen, like some of the women you have already read about, was an ardent follower of Gandhi. She participated actively in his Quit India Movement in 1942. On Independence Day in 1972, the Indian prime minister honoured Helen with the Tamra Patra, an award for freedom fighters. Helen lived simply and privately during her later years. Fondly remembered as 'the daughter of the soil' in her birth state, Sikkim, Helen lived a fearless life and fought for the freedom of the country and its people, particularly those belonging to the working class.

# BIBHA CHOWDHURI

## A Star Named Bibha

Every night, a small yellowish-white star named Bibha keeps twinkling in a constellation, far far away from our solar system. Earlier, it was called HD86081. Astronomers commonly use numbers and letters to denote stars. Only on rare occasions do they name stars after some very special human beings. In 2019, the International Astronomical Union, the most revered global organization that reasearches planets and stars, named a star 'Bibha'. They wanted to honour the forgotten Indian scientist Bibha Chowdhuri, who remained far from the limelight during her lifetime. Isn't it a coincidence that the word 'Bibha' means 'a beam of light' in Sanskrit?

Bibha Chowdhuri was born in 1913 to Urmila Devi and Bankubihari Chowdhuri, a doctor by profession. While Bankubihari hailed from a prosperous and traditional family in Hooghly, Urmila Devi belonged to a modern Brahmo family in Bengal. Bibha was sent to Bethune School in North Calcutta. She was a bright student and enjoyed studying. After completing school, she joined Scottish Church College in Calcutta and thereafter the University of Calcutta. In those days, girls were married off early and very few of them could study this far. Bibha was the only woman in a class of twenty-four students when she was pursuing a Master's in physics. It was a common misconception that women did not have the intellect to study hard science disciplines, like maths and physics. Even today, we find relatively few women in these fields because of such mindsets. But Bibha challenged this mindset by going on to become a researcher in experimental physics.

Bibha approached Debendra Mohan Bose, a celebrated professor of physics at the University of Calcutta, hoping to be included in his research team at the Bose Institute, a premier place for physics research in India. Bose, who was also her brother-in-law, was initially reluctant to let her in and said that there were no positions suitable for women in his team. After a lot of effort, Bibha managed to convince Bose to grant her entry into his team. There were many men like Bose in those days. Even the Nobel Laureate physicist C.V. Raman was no different. He was unwilling to grant admission to a brilliant and determined student, Kamala Sohonie, to the Indian Institute of Science, since he believed that women were not capable of doing research.

At the Bose Institute, Bibha made path breaking discoveries with D.M. Bose. They published their findings in the world-renowned journal *Nature*. Unfortunately, they could not continue this research because the equipment that was necessary for their experiments became unavailable during the Second World War (1939–45). A few years later, the English physicist C.F. Powell was awarded the Nobel Prize in physics for doing similar work. Powell mentioned the works of Bibha Chowdhuri in his writings. When Bibha had to discontinue her work at the Bose Institute, she joined the University of Manchester in the United Kingdom for her doctoral research in the laboratory of the world-renowned physicist P.M.S. Blackett. They worked together on a new topic, for which Blackett was later awarded the Nobel Prize.

After completing her doctoral research, Bibha returned to India and joined the Tata Institute of Fundamental Research in Bombay, which the famous scientist Homi Bhabha was then setting up. In the next four decades, she worked at premier science institutes in India with leading scientists as colleagues. She made important contributions and kept publishing her research until her death in 1991.

An introvert with few friends, Bibha dedicated her life to the pursuit of science. She chose to remain unmarried, and little is known about her personal life. In an interview to *The Manchester Herald*, titled 'Meet India's New Woman Scientist – She has an eye for cosmic rays', she said, 'In this age when science, and physics particularly, is more important than ever, women should study atomic power; if they don't understand how it works, how can they help decide how it should be used?' She believed that women suffered much during wars, and it was their right to know if governments misused deadly weapons using atomic power.

    Scientists today lament that Bibha did not get her due recognition in her lifetime. The scientific world of those days could not come to terms with the exceptional brilliance of a woman. She was not even made a member of the leading scientific societies of India. S.C. Bhattacharya, a famous scientist who became the director of the Bose Institute, is known to have said, 'D.M. Bose should have offered the directorship of Bose Institute to Bibhadi instead of offering it to me.'

# SARALA THAKRAL

## With Wings to Fly

Looking at aeroplanes zooming high up in the sky, many of us wish we could fly. Sarala, a girl from Delhi, perhaps had similar dreams. Her life made it possible for many little girls to achieve their dreams of flying an aeroplane. Sarala Thakral was born in 1914. At the age of sixteen, she was married to P.D. Sharma and moved to Lahore, where she lived with his family. Her husband's family was full of pilots. At the time of her marriage, there were nine pilots in the family! They encouraged Sarala to learn flying. Her father-in-law, in fact, enrolled her in the local flying school. This was rather unusual at a time when families wanted to keep their daughters and daughters-in-law inside the house.

Sarala turned out to be a natural. On the very first day of her training, after flying for a mere eight hours, her instructor allowed her to fly alone. She flew a Gypsy Moth plane, taking it to the required altitude and then landing the plane on her own. These planes were wooded, two-seater, with wings that could be folded. At a time when aeroplanes were flown only by men, Sarala went on to earn her 'A' license at the age of twenty-one and flew for over 1,000 hours. She was by then a mother to a four-year-old daughter.

In 1939, Sarala's husband died in a plane crash. This tragic accident made her withdraw from training for a commercial flying license. But she had two young daughters to support. So, eventually, she went to Jodhpur to complete her training to be a commercial pilot. But soon, the Second World War broke out. At that time India was under British occupation and had to get involved in the war as a colony. Commercial flying was suspended to direct all efforts towards the war. Sarala could not obtain her license. She was disappointed. But she needed to be self-reliant for her and her daughters' sake. Sarala then decided to give up on her dream of flying planes. She enrolled in Mayo School of Arts in Lahore and studied painting. She also mastered handicraft, calligraphy and costume jewellery designing. From here began the second phase of her career, when she became a businesswoman.

Sarala continued to live in Lahore till 1947 and ran a successful business there. The independence of India in 1947 came with the partition of the subcontinent. The birth of the two new countries, India and Pakistan, was accompanied by killing and violence. Much of the violence on both sides of the border was along religious lines. Sarala's Muslim neighbours worried about her safety as she was a Hindu. They advised her to leave for India with her daughters. She took a train with her daughters and headed back to Delhi, her birthplace. Here she met R.P. Thakral, whom she married in 1948.

Sarala restarted her business of designing costume jewellery and selling it. She even designed saris. Her work was very popular. She had many famous clients such as Vijaya Lakshmi Pandit, an important Indian politician. Even though she could not pursue her first career choice, she did not lose hope. She pursued a successful second career. Her jewellery was bought by many important shops like the Costume Emporium for fifteen years. She also designed jewellery for the National School of Drama in Delhi. Sarala believed that growing old should not mean becoming frail. So, even in her advanced years, she remained self-reliant, continuing her business and doing her own housework.

Today, India has the highest number of women commercial pilots in the world, double the worldwide numbers. This was made possible by the twenty-one-year-old sari-clad woman who fearlessly climbed into the cockpit of a plane—a place where no Indian woman before her had ventured—and took command of the flight. She could not fulfil her dream, but she took the first steps towards making it possible for other women to achieve the dream of flying and soaring high. Sarala

Thakral, however, was more than the first Indian woman to fly a plane. Her story highlights the importance of conquering disappointment and obstacles by remaining dependent on no one but oneself.

# A. LALITHA

Engineering Social Change

Pappu Subba Rao, a professor at an engineering college, loved his children dearly. He wanted his daughters and sons to be equally educated. When Ayyalasomayajula Lalitha, more commonly known as A. Lalitha, turned fifteen in 1934, Subba Rao fixed her marriage according to the social norm of the time. While doing so, he and his wife ensured that Lalitha would be able to continue her studies even after marriage. Lalitha herself was also very interested in her studies. She passed the secondary school exam with flying colours. She was also happy in her marriage. Lalitha gave birth to her daughter, Syamala, when she was eighteen. Little did she know that a great tragedy awaited her. Four months after Syamala was born, Lalitha lost her husband.

Life is not easy for single mothers and widows even today. In those days, the difficulties were almost insurmountable for women like Lalitha. Luckily, her family firmly stood by her. Lalitha believed that she could lead a dignified life on her own terms only if she educated herself well. She passed the intermediate examination with first class. She then considered becoming a doctor, since she knew of some women, like Muthulakshmi, who had studied medicine. However, after some thought, she decided to get a degree in engineering, like her father.

The College of Engineering at Guindy in Madras, which Lalitha wished to join, admitted only male students. At that time, few women opted for the discipline of engineering. But Pappu Subba Rao was a progressive thinker. He encouraged his brilliant daughter and requested his colleague, the principal of the college, Dr K.C. Chacko, to admit Lalitha in the four-year electrical engineering course. Dr Chacko too was a man ahead of his time. He ensured the admission of the first female student of engineering in the country to his college.

Lalitha studied hard in college. She stayed in a separate hostel that was arranged for her and would visit her daughter every weekend. However, she was lonely in college. The male students looked at her in awe, and some of them did not approve of a woman entering a 'men's' field. It was the first half of the twentieth century, and friendship between male and female students was not acceptable in society. Pappu Subba Rao wanted Lalitha to be not only successful but also happy. He posted an advertisement asking more women to join the college. It was an important moment in history when two other women, P.K. Thresia and Leelamma George, joined the college. The three ladies became friends and enjoyed each other's company.

## A. LALITHA

Lalitha became the first Indian woman to receive a degree in electronics engineering in 1943. Everyone who passed with Honours received a certificate signed by the vice-chancellor of the University of Madras. Typed in cursive font, it looked elegant and included the sentence, 'He passed the examination with Honours'. An exception had to be made for Lalitha. The word 'He' was replaced with a handwritten 'She', and history was made.

After graduating, Lalitha took up a job as an engineering assistant in Shimla. She stayed with her brother. Her sister-in-law looked after Syamala when she was away at work. After two years, she left this job and started assisting her father, her idol, in his research on steamless ovens. No matter how much she enjoyed her job, she needed to earn more to raise Syamala. She took up a new job in Calcutta, where another of her brothers stayed. She could not go and work in a city of her choice since it was extremely difficult for a single woman with a child to live alone. Therefore, she always chose a city where she had some family members to help her with Syamala.

A. Lalitha earned many accolades in life. In independent India, she worked as an engineer to build the nation's largest dam, the Bhakra Nangal Dam.

She was invited by organizations in other countries such as the United Kingdom and the United States of America. At a prestigious conference held in New York in 1964, she said, 'Hundred fifty years ago, I would have been burnt at the funeral pyre with my husband's body.' She was referring to the Hindu custom of sati, which forced a widow to jump into the burning pyre of her dead husband. Indeed the times had changed and now a widow could become an engineer! It was women like Lalitha who made this change happen.

# CHAKALI ILAMMA

## For Her Land and Dignity

There once lived a woman called Chakali Ilamma in the princely state of Hyderabad. She was born on 10 September 1919 to Oruganti Mallamma and Soilu. Chakali was the fourth of their five children. Ilamma's family belonged to the Rajak caste, considered a low caste. The Rajaks were supposed to wash the clothes of the upper-caste zamindars whom they served. Oruganti and Soilu were very poor. They could not send Ilamma and her siblings to school. Ilamma was married off as a child. She and her husband too continued the work assigned to their caste of washing clothes to earn their living. But Ilamma did not want this kind of life. She wanted to be free from the control of the zamindars and earn her living with dignity. Thus began her fight for land and food.

Ilamma wanted to own land where she and her family could grow their own crops. She leased forty acres of land from a zamindar named Kondala Rao to cultivate it. This caused a great stir in the region. At that time, it was unthinkable that a woman, that too from a lower caste, would cultivate her own land. The upper-caste landlords and the ruler of Hyderabad, the Nizam, were all shocked. They decided to teach Ilamma a lesson. The Nizam's officials were sent to ask her to give up her land and instead work in others' fields. Ilamma refused. The angry zamindars then sent their men to beat her and her family. Brave Ilamma was not afraid; she told them: 'This is my land. This is my crop. Who is this Dora [upper-caste landlords] to take away my land and crop? It is only possible for you when I die.' Realizing that she would not be scared off, the most powerful zamindar in the region, Visnoor Deshmukh, filed a false case against her and her family. Her husband and son were arrested by the police. But Ilamma fought the false case in court and rescued her family.

Defeated by her courage, the zamindars decided to punish her. Visnoor Deshmukh ordered that her house be burnt to the ground. With the help of a government servant, Deshmukh's men burnt down her house and attacked her husband and daughter. This was a brutal act against a woman who was only fighting to protect her own land and crops. Ilamma was not a violent woman, but she knew that if she kept quiet, there could be more attacks and poor people like her would continue to suffer. She destroyed the patwari's house as a symbol of evil and cultivated corn on that land. Instead of the wicked and the powerful, the cornfield was to be for all, including the poor, lower caste and downtrodden. Politically aware and active, Ilamma was a member of the Andhra Mahasabha, a people's organization spearheading a movement for the rights of the poor in the state of Hyderabad. This act of making land and crops available for all inspired the Communist Party of India.

This led to a movement in Telangana where riches and crops were taken from landlords and given back to the poor. The violence and selfishness of the upper-caste zamindars and the government was finally defeated through the courage and inclusiveness of Ilamma's action.

Ilamma and her comrades also fought for Hyderabad's freedom from the evil clutches of the Nizam's government in 1947. This is known as the Telangana Armed Rebellion. Resisting the armed forces of the landlords and the Nizam, this movement was successful in ending illegal taxes and grain collections and reclaiming land taken away by the zamindars.

Ilamma's fight to cultivate her own land was not just a fight for forty acres, it was a fight for dignity for all low-caste poor people like her. She also strongly criticized the many ways in which the upper caste tried to humiliate people from the lower castes. She challenged upper-caste women who insisted that lower-caste women call them 'Dora', an address meant to establish their authority. She asked how upper-caste women were superior to women like her. Her struggle encouraged many women. She was one of the earliest women to raise her voice against the tyranny of upper-caste zamindars, the Nizam and the British government. Instead of mutely accepting the life handed to her, she became a prominent leader of the people and a voice against oppression of any kind. In spite of all her achievements, Chakali Ilamma remains forgotten in history and her contributions are largely ignored. It was only as late as 2018 that the Telangana government installed her statue in Warangal to honour her role in the freedom movement. Women like Chakali Ilamma fought against caste and patriarchy to try to make the world we live in a better, more equal place.

# AMRITA PRITAM
## The Poet of Partition

In the historic city of Lahore lived Amrita, a young Punjabi poet. Born in 1919 to a mother who was a schoolteacher and a father who was also a poet, Amrita started writing at a very young age. When she was only thirteen, one of her poems was published for the first time. Within three years, she began to receive fame and attention as a poet in Punjabi society.

When Amrita was in her twenties, the world around her began to change rapidly. The Second World War killed millions and destroyed large parts of Europe and parts of East Asia. India was dragged into the war as the Japanese army invaded its eastern frontier. The country witnessed a famine because of the wartime economic policies of the British Raj. Soon after the war, India became independent from the British in 1947. But with independence came the partition. British India was divided into two separate countries – India and Pakistan. This was a dreadful chapter in the subcontinent's history. People killed each other in the name of religion. Punjab, now divided between India and Pakistan, saw the most brutal violence.

All these events shaped Amrita's poems. In 1944, she wrote *Lok Peer* (People's Pain), which was about the famine. She became associated with the Progressive Writers' Movement around this time. The writers that were part of the movement spoke against inequality in the society and wrote about Hindu-Muslim friendship. Amrita's writings became more political and courageous during this period. But it was the partition that had the most effect on her writings. She left Lahore, a Pakistani city, after partition and moved to Delhi with her husband, Pritam Singh. All around her, she saw riots and devastation. In her poems, she expressed her sorrow and pain. Perhaps her best poems were written around this time, including the very famous 'Ajj aakhaan Waris Shah nu' (Today I call upon Waris Shah). This poem was about the sufferings of Punjabi women during the time of partition. It became very famous among Punjabi speakers across India and Pakistan. Amrita wrote a novel, *Pinjar*, to capture the realities of partition. The novel was later made into a popular Hindi film.

Amrita dreamt and wrote of a society where women and men would be equal and women would be free. Many of her poems and short stories highlighted the troubles faced by women in families and in marriages. She also wrote about women's needs and desires. Amrita herself lived life on her own terms. At that time, divorces were rare. Society expected women to stay in a marriage even if it was an unhappy one. But Amrita did not fear society. She left her husband as he could not appreciate her love for poetry and did not like her poetry-reading sessions on the radio. Though divorced, they remained in touch, and Amrita took care of him in his last days. Amrita then lived with Imroz, a young painter, who was a great admirer of her work. Though they never got married, they shared a beautiful relationship built on admiration and affection. Together they published *Nagmani*, a literary journal, for thirty-six years. Like Imroz, Amrita found an admirer in Sahir Ludhianvi, a famous poet of the time. They had deep love and respect for each other. Though their relationship did not take the conventional route of marriage, their admiration for each other influenced their prose and poetry.

Amrita's life and writings were criticized by many conservatives. She wrote too openly about the man-woman relationship, they complained. Her short hair, a divorce and the habit of smoking did not go down well with conservative people. But her talent was recognized by many. Her poems, novels and short stories brought Amrita many awards and much appreciation. She was the first woman to win the prestigious Sahitya Akademi Award in 1956. Later, she also received the Padma Shri, the Jnanpith Award and the Padma Vibhushan for her contributions to Punjabi literature. Amrita's writings were translated into many languages across the world.

She received literary awards from the French and Bulgarian governments. It was through her work that Punjabi literature received the attention of the entire world.

Amrita received a lot of love and admiration from Pakistan. Among her admirers were great poets like Faiz Ahmed Faiz, learned men and women and common people too. A poor fruit-seller from Pakistan once sent some fruits to Amrita after reading her poems. When she was unwell, a group of Pakistani writers collected chaddars (holy cloth) from various shrines of religious saints and sent them to her house. Amrita, however, never visited Lahore after migrating to India. She did not want to remember the violence she saw in Lahore during partition. The partitioned society of India and Pakistan found comfort in Amrita's writings. Her poetry, stories and novels brought the people of these two countries close amidst the ruins of partition. Reading Amrita is therefore a celebration of love, friendship and peace. Amrita's writings stand for freedom, love and humanity in times of suffering.

# VIDYA MUNSHI

## Breaking Barriers for Breaking News

A tall, young woman with bright, bespectacled eyes jumped off an eight-foot wall to avoid the policemen who were chasing her in a crowded street of Calcutta. Thousands of teachers had gathered to demonstrate against the government. She had gone to meet these teachers. The first page of the next day's newspaper that she worked for would carry a report signed off by her. So she knew that she had to escape the police. This was Vidya, arguably India's first woman journalist. Ever since she'd returned from England, her days had been filled with thrill and excitement.

Vidya Kanuga was born to a prosperous Gujarati family in 1919. Her father was a renowned lawyer. He inspired Vidya to read. She stood first among women in the school-leaving examination. After this, she wanted to go to England to study medicine. When some of her family members protested against the idea of a girl going abroad for studies, her maternal grandmother stood by her. She said that since Vidya had the courage, it would be wrong to deny her the chance to do what she wanted in life.

In England, Vidya joined the Communist Party of Great Britain, a political organization that believed in equal rights for all human beings. In 1945, she participated in a women's conference in Paris.

These experiences made her think deeply about the miseries of the underprivileged. By then she had decided that she would not study medicine. She wanted to become a journalist. In those days, it was not an easy choice. There were no women in the field of journalism, neither reporters nor editors. Moreover, Vidya wanted to do investigative journalism, a genre that required energy and tenacity. It meant taking up a job that would require solving mysteries, chasing miscreants and writing about their crimes. Brave, witty and hardworking, Vidya was willing to take up the challenge.

When she returned from England, she married her friend, Sunil Munshi, a famous geographer, who edited the journal *The Student*. Vidya trained herself to become a reporter during her stint at this journal. She even learnt Bengali when she was suddenly asked to edit a Bengali magazine. Later, she worked for the *Blitz Weekly*, which was the best paper to work for if one wanted to do investigative journalism. While working for the *Blitz*, she broke many exciting stories. She earned a lot of fame when she wrote a report about two Canadian pilots who flew from Hong Kong and dropped stolen gold on a remote island in the Sunderbans in West Bengal. This gold was to be smuggled into Calcutta. She was the first reporter to write about a heartbreaking disaster in a mine in Chinakuri in West Bengal. Hundreds of workers lost their lives in this tragic incident. Based on her report, the famous playwright Utpal Dutt wrote the acclaimed play *Angar*.

    Vidya Munshi believed in equal rights for all human beings and was vocal about it throughout her life. She wrote profusely about the rights of women, who in those days were not free to make their own choices in life. Women are often barred from choosing a profession of their choice, even today. Even when they work, they are sometimes denied their due wages. Many women face problems inside their homes. Those days, it was not common to talk about these problems. Vidya was aggrieved by these issues and all through her life she fought for the rights of women and the underprivileged. She took part in protests and even headed the State Women's Commission, a body that looked into offences against women. She visited many countries to study and discuss the problems faced by women. Vidya Munshi wrote about her experiences in a book titled *In Retrospect: War-time Memories and Thoughts on Women's Movement*. The book, published in 2006, described important movements in world politics, which she witnessed over a span of seventy years.

    Vidya suffered from a cerebral stroke when she was

ninety. After this, she could not move the right side of her body. Even then she did not stop working. She would take notes with her left hand. With a failing eyesight, she had to use a magnifying glass to read. Her colleagues, who affectionately called her 'Vidyadi', fondly recall how nothing could dampen her spirit. Vidya Munshi died on 8 July 2014. The world today, still plagued by injustices against women and the underprivileged, surely needs more women like Vidya Munshi.

# SULAGITTI NARASAMMA
## The Mother of All

India is a country of high birth mortality, which means that many babies die at the time of birth. Experts say that this is because good and safe healthcare does not reach all mothers and their soon-to-be-born children. In a country like ours, the role of a woman who single-handedly delivered over 15,000 babies is very important. This woman is Narasamma, popularly known as Sulagitti Narasamma.

Narasamma was born in 1920 in Pavagada village in Karnataka. She belonged to a nomadic tribe who were considered 'untouchable', that is, low caste. Hailing from a poor family, Narasamma did not get the chance to go to school. But from a young age, she was a keen observer and learner. Married at the tender age of twelve, Narasamma learnt the traditional art of delivering babies from her grandmother, Marigemma. Such knowledge was not commonly available. Marigemma delivered five of Narasamma's children. It was at the age of twenty that Narasamma first helped deliver a baby, and she continued doing this work tirelessly for seven decades.

Narasamma's work earned her the title 'Sulagitti', which is a Kannada word for midwife, or someone trained to assist women in childbirth. Why was her work important? In rural Karnataka, there were many villages and communities which were totally cut off from modern hospitals and doctors as well as roads. Hospital deliveries were not common in those days. Unassisted births were dangerous for the mother and the newborn baby. In these situations, Narasamma's skill as a midwife saved many lives. While there were other midwives in the region, most women preferred her. Like her grandmother, she was considered special in her abilities. She had a talent for checking the pulse of the foetus and the position of its head without any instrument. Most of the women were poor like Sulagitti. So she did not take any money from them for her services. Instead, she considered herself a protector of these women. We do not know what motivated Sulagitti or why she, despite being poor herself, chose not to charge others. But it was clear that she was passionate about her work. And all through her long life, she continued this along with her work in the fields.

    Narasamma was not satisfied with the basic midwifery skills that she'd developed. She wanted to learn more so that she could do her job better. She wanted to know how to keep babies healthy. She learnt about natural remedies and traditional practices from the nomadic tribes who frequented her village. Her commitment was towards both the babies and their mothers. She made Ayurvedic medicine for new mothers to ease their pain or other difficulties after they had given birth. Her work shows how she successfully combined her natural skills with traditional knowledge and a scientific temper.

Narasamma served her community at a time when traditional midwives were discredited. The British government promoted allopathic medical practices and opposed the traditional profession of Indian midwives. They said that such women were illiterate and had no knowledge about allopathic medicine. The educated middle class claimed that rural midwives were almost like witches who caused babies to die. It is true that sometimes the label of indigenousness or tradition is used to pass off superstitions and unscientific—even dangerous—methods as knowledge. That is why practitioners of modern science often distrust indigenous knowledge systems. But the kind of work Narasamma did in delivering babies and looking after new mothers was not altogether different from the foundations of modern science. It was also based on the same scientific understanding of the human body and of birth. These practices were based on generations of knowledge that women from a nomadic culture had acquired, not from magic and superstition, but from close observation of nature and animals, and ecology and humans.

At this juncture in history, Narasamma's work was of immense importance. In remote areas with no hospitals or doctors, and mostly poor people and a lack of midwives, her skill and knowledge helped in reducing infant mortality. Her selfless work helped in creating alternative avenues of childbirth. She taught her skills to a group of one hundred and eighty students, including one of her daughters, so that the knowledge could be preserved. In 2018, at the age of ninety-two, Narasamma died of a lung infection. Her faith in traditional knowledge and natural remedies was not unscientific. Sulagitti Narasamma's work has now been recognized through multiple awards, including a Padma Shri. She also needs to be remembered for understanding the scientific value of knowledge cultivated by ancient nomadic communities and putting it to use along with science.

# URMILA EULIE CHOWDHURY

## Brick by Brick, Block by Block

Once there was a man called Le Corbusier, who was very famous for building beautiful houses and planning great cities across the world. In India, he built Chandigarh. There were young Indian architects in his team that worked in Chandigarh. They helped him and learnt from him. Among them was a twenty-eight-year-old girl named Urmila Eulie. She was one of Asia and India's first trained female architects. Perin Mistri, a Parsi woman from Bombay, was another practising architect who was her contemporary.

Urmila Eulie Chowdhury was born in Shahjehanpur, Uttar Pradesh on 4 October 1923. Her father was a diplomat. Eulie travelled with him to different countries. She did her schooling from Japan. Then she went to Australia to study architecture. Next, she moved to the United States to learn how to make pots and pans with clay. She also learnt music. While she was lucky to have a globetrotting father who wanted the best education for his daughter, her own hard work made her a successful architect.

In 1951, when Eulie was in the States, the opportunity to join Corbusier's Chandigarh team came up. India was then a newly independent nation, and Jawaharlal Nehru, the first prime minister, wanted bright, young Indian minds to work for the development of the country. Eulie, a patriot at heart, took up the challenge and came back to India.

From 1951 to 1981, Eulie mostly stayed and worked in Chandigarh as a part of Corbusier's team. After that, Eulie became the chief state architect of Haryana and then of Punjab. In between, she was briefly the director of the School of Planning and Architecture, New Delhi (1863–1965). If you ever go to Chandigarh, remember to visit the Home Science College and the Women's Polytechnic College. Both these institutions were designed by Eulie. Eulie also designed the residences of the ministers in Chandigarh, government schools, flats for government employees and hostels for students. Though she was trained abroad, she did not blindly copy European designs. She paid great attention to the climate of Chandigarh. She knew that the buildings that suited the European climate might not be suitable for India. Moreover, she was good at designing low-cost furniture, suitable for a newly independent country that did not have much money. All the wooden furniture of the government offices in Chandigarh and the Punjab University was designed by her. Eulie's designs were simple, functional and cost-effective. She received a gold medal in 1954 from the president of India for her beautiful yet affordable furniture designs. Eulie was known for her command over French. This came in handy when she was working with Le Corbusier. The master architect did not speak English fluently and very few in India could understand French. Eulie acted as the mediator between Corbusier and his Indian associates. She was also the mediator between Nehru and Corbusier, and translated their correspondence regularly. After she retired from her post as the chief state architect of Punjab, she helped to establish the Alliance Française in Chandigarh, where the residents could learn her favourite language.

Eulie was disciplined, punctual and hardworking. When she was at work, she met people only if they had prior appointments. She always wore a stern expression when she was in the office. In those days, very few women held high official posts and their male colleagues did not always treat them with due respect. That is why, perhaps, Eulie had to be strict and sombre at work. Outside the office, however, she was great fun. Eulie loved the theatre and founded the Chandigarh Amateur Dramatic Society, where English plays were staged. With Eulie, a slice of Europe came to Chandigarh.

Eulie regularly wrote witty articles in the Saturday supplement of *The Tribune*, a daily newspaper of Chandigarh. She wrote about interesting people and shared anecdotes about the city. Eulie contributed frequently to another column, 'Sinners and Winners', highlighting the mistakes and incorrect information that *The Tribune* had unknowingly published. In addition, she wrote serious pieces in various journals of architecture and translated Corbusier's writings into English. She also wrote a memoir about her own experiences with Corbusier in Chandigarh.

Architecture has always been a man's world. In 2020, there were only seventeen women in every hundred architects in the United States. In India there are more than forty-seven women in every hundred architects. Unfortunately though, only one out of five registered Indian women architects actually practise the profession. Eulie was an exception. Her legacy lives on in the buildings she built, the furniture she designed and the books and articles she wrote. May her tribe increase and expand!

# MEERA MUKHERJEE

## The Sculptor of the Every Day

Meera Mukherjee was born in Calcutta to Dwijendramohan Mukherjee and Binapani Devi in 1923. Little Meera was very interested in learning art. At the age of fourteen, she was enrolled in the Indian Society of Oriental Art, which was started by the famous painter Abanindranath Tagore. She studied there for four years till she got married. But hers was not a happy marriage and ended soon. Meera did not let this deter her. She decided to pursue her dream of learning different art forms and earned a diploma from Delhi Polytechnic. Meera was a talented artist, but she felt she still had much to learn. So she went to Munich in Germany on a scholarship in 1953 to study painting. After the first term, she decided to drop painting and take up sculpting, the art of making statues by carving, modelling or casting. She was not afraid of changing careers.

Meera's teacher, Toni Stadler, was very strict and was not happy with her work. Meera was always thinking about ways to improve. One night, after months of sleeplessness, she took a small piece of wood and crafted a bowl out of it. This was the first of her trademark styles. This came to be known as the process of 'identification', in which the artist did not draw inspiration from outside but from their own self and mood. This bowl also won her praise from her teacher and other students.

Meera could have stayed on in Germany and built a career there. But she decided to come back to India and learn from the traditional artists of the country. The tribal artists of India were master sculptors. But they did not get any recognition. In fact, the upper castes of society often looked down on the tribal communities and their art. But Meera realized how valuable these were. She wanted to learn from them. She took up teaching jobs at a few schools to earn money. Once she'd made some money she went on a tour to visit the tribal heartlands in central India. From the Gonds of Dandakaranya, to Bastar Gharuas to Nepali Sakya metal workers, she was awestruck by the range of art in these communities. The tribals of Bastar were skilled artists of dokra. Meera stayed with them to study their craft. She combined the traditional dokra technique with her training in Germany and created her own trademark style. This style of sculpting on bronze earned her great fame. Her experience in learning art in Bastar also taught her to understand the craft in a new way. Her real teachers were these ordinary men and women who worked in the fields and made statues and paintings. It was from them that she learnt the dokra technique. They were ordinary men and women who worked in the fields and made statues and paintings. She learnt hard work, humility and techniques of sculpting from these masters. She once wrote: 'I have learnt from them—their life and craft—their craft entirely embraces and encompasses their life.'

Along with being a sculptor, Meera was a writer. She wrote and illustrated many children's books. She also worked to preserve kantha embroidery. She trained a group of young girls in kantha work and collaborated closely with carpet weavers and artisans. She encouraged young children to study handicraft. As a socially aware person, Meera secured education and employment for many craftspeople, especially women. Meera loved music, and her passion for it is visible in her sculptures. She took lessons in both Rabindra Sangeet and German classical music. She often made figurines of various instrument players. She could produce movement even on bronze.

Meera Mukherjee was an extraordinary painter of the ordinary. Her art drew from the very heart of traditional folk art of India. She drew ordinary people at their ordinary work. While we will never learn the names of the masters in Bastar she learnt from, her art and life is a tribute to them. She decided that she was not an artist but one who created works of art: 'If I am an ordinary human being, then I will continue to do ordinary chores and remain satisfied and happy with it. I did not have an enormous ambition; I did not wish to become a great artist. Whatever be my standard, as a human being, I will only desire that which I feel good about.' She received many government awards and much praise for her outstanding work and unique style. She died in 1998. Meera Mukherjee's work and life teach us the richness of tribal art in India and the exquisite beauty of the ordinary.

# SHANTABAI KAMBLE

The Touching Life Story of an
Untouchable Woman

Naja was born in Maharashtra in 1923 to a very poor family of Mahars, one of the largest Dalit communities in the state. Her father's name was Sakharam Babar. Her mother was called Gavalabai. Both her parents worked in the fields as labourers. They toiled hard but earned very little money. The family often went hungry and even ate leftover cattle feed to fill their stomachs. Naja was born after three daughters. Her father was very upset at her birth since he had wanted a son. But Naja's mother was a strong woman. Seeing her interest in studies, Naja's mother would always inspire her to read. When the girls of their family were treated badly by their in-laws, Gavalabai supported them and fought for them.

When Naja was in Class 3, the headmaster of her school said she would receive a scholarship of three rupees every month from the government. He told her to study hard. The scholarship would be stopped if she failed in her exams, he said. So, Naja studied relentlessly. When girls in her class laughed at her for her worn-out clothes, Naja would feel sad and humiliated. As in Parbatibai's times, the schools were not yet happy places for a poor Dalit child like Naja. Naja's mother would tell her repeatedly that she could have a better life only by studying hard. Naja wanted to support her parents and end their misery when she grew up.

When Naja was in Class 5, she was the only girl in her class. This was because students in her school received vocational education from Class 5. Girls dropped out from school since it was believed that they did not need to learn carpentry or the work of an ironsmith. However, in Class 6, a new girl called Shaku joined Naja's school. Shaku and Naja became great friends. One day, Shaku didn't come to school. The headmaster sent Naja to Shaku's house to find out why she had been absent. Seeing Naja standing outside the door, Shaku's mother shouted, 'You, daughter of a Mahar, do not step inside!' Shaku was a Brahmin. Naja did not forget those insulting words all her life.

When Naja was in Class 7, the kind headmaster of the school was transferred. The new headmaster called her and asked her to take admission in a girls' school that was far from their house. Naja had to discontinue her studies. Meanwhile, their relatives started bringing marriage proposals for her. Her father and brother rejected proposals from wealthier families. Instead, they wanted a schoolteacher as Naja's husband, who could help her to continue her studies.

Finally, a match was found for Naja. The groom was a schoolteacher called Kamble Master. In those days, girls had little say in their marriages. Kamble Master saw

Naja and wanted to marry her. Nobody asked Naja if she wanted to marry him. When he demanded a dowry, Naja's brother said, 'Will you send us her salary when she becomes a schoolteacher?' This was highly unusual at that time. After marriage, women were considered outsiders to their maternal families.

After marriage, Naja was called Shantabai Krishnaji Kamble. Kamble Master was a good teacher but a bad husband. He deceived Shantabai and married again. Shantabai came back to her father's house and took up a teaching job. However, after some time she went back to her husband. Despite difficulties, she stayed in the marriage. Kamble Master later supported her work and helped her family. Shantabai had children with him. To her agony, some of them died in infancy. Two sons and a daughter survived. All of them grew up to be well-educated.

Shantabai underwent a teacher's training course and taught in different schools. She supported her parents and siblings with her own money. She met the great Dalit leader Babasaheb Ambedkar in 1942 and was deeply inspired by his ideas. She joined his movement and converted to Buddhism. She worked with her husband to spread awareness among people about the evils of the caste system.

After retirement, Shantabai wrote the story of her life in Marathi. Titled *Majya Jalmachi Chittarkatha*, the book has since been translated into English and French. It was even made into a television serial in Marathi. This was the first autobiography written by a Dalit woman in India. In those days, the society did not give women, particularly Dalit women, any importance. Women were seen as inferior to men. Through her story, Shantabai questioned this mindset. She wrote about herself because she knew her life and struggles were important enough for the world to read. Her writings became her way to change the society's mindset.

# FATIMA BEEVI

## Raising the Bar

Since India became independent, only eleven women have served as judges of the Supreme Court. It was Fatima Beevi who, many years ago, broke the glass ceiling to become the first woman judge.

Fatima was born in 1927 in the princely state of Travancore, now a part of Kerala. She was the eldest of six daughters and two sons. Her father, Annaveetil Meera Sahib, was in government service. He was very particular about the education of all his children. After completing her schooling from Catholicate High School in 1943, Fatima went to Trivandrum for higher studies. She studied science and completed B.Sc. successfully. Her plan was to continue studying science. But her father had other ideas. He wanted his daughter to pursue a career in law. The Indian court system is a triangular structure. There is a district court in every district above the subsidiary courts. Above the district court is the high court, the top court in every state. Above the high court is the Supreme Court, the apex court of India. Fatima's father was inspired by the life of Justice Anna Chandi. Chandi was the first woman judge of India in a district court and later became a high court judge in 1959. Fatima's father came to know of Anna Chandi's work because her office was near their house. This made him think of a similar path for his brilliant daughter. He told her that an M.Sc. degree would lead her to the beaten path of teaching and living in Trivandrum. Studying law, on the other hand, would take her on a journey to new places. Fatima was inspired by her father's vision and decided to study law.

Fatima was one of the five women students in her law course. During the course, the number dropped to three. It was clear that studying law was hardly seen as an option among women at that time. But Fatima remained determined. She obtained a law degree in 1950. After that she sat for the Bar Council examination, a test that law graduates have to take to practise law in India. She topped this examination and won a gold medal – the first woman to do so. But she was to make more history.

Fatima started her career as an advocate in Kerala. She faced much opposition from people who were displeased at the presence of a head-scarfed woman at the district court in Kollam, Kerala. This was a time when people were not used to seeing women as advocates, and a Muslim woman lawyer was even more uncommon. People were conditioned to think that Muslim families were more conservative in allowing their daughters to pursue such careers. But Fatima's career choices and family support helped in breaking such preconceived notions.

# FATIMA BEEVI

Though Fatima worked as an advocate for eight years, she gradually realized that it was difficult for women to practise as they were not encouraged by the general public. But Fatima was not one to give up. She decided to go a notch higher and try for judicial service. So, from being an advocate who argued a case in court, she now wanted to become a judge who would listen to these arguments and decide the outcome of a case. She wrote another examination, this time for the lowest judiciary of the state. She passed and was appointed as a munsiff, the lowest judicial officer. As a munsiff, she handled several cases. She was polite, balanced in her judgments and always well-prepared for a case. Her brilliance and dedication made her rise through the ranks and earn the respect of others. After several promotions, she became a judge in the Kerala High Court in 1983. She handled cases of riots and murders, and her judgments were of great importance.

In 1986, she became the first woman to be appointed as a judge in the Supreme Court in India. Fatima Beevi knew how difficult it was for women to reach this level. She was vocal about the opposition that women like her faced from society. It was not the absence of qualified women but the negative attitude of society which prevented women from taking up the legal profession.

She advocated the reservation of women in the higher ranks of the judiciary.

Fatima Beevi's illustrious career did not end with her retirement from the Supreme Court in 1992. She served as a member of the National Human Rights Commission and the chairman of Kerala Commission for Backward Classes in 1993. Fatima Beevi's life and career was thus not just about remarkable achievements. It was also about improving the system and the society. Even today, when we are celebrating over seven decades of independence, the Indian judiciary, especially the Supreme Court, hesitates to open its gates to women judges. It is remarkable that Fatima Beevi challenged this attitude and entered this pillar of Indian democracy. She remains an inspiration to young girls who seek to enter the male-dominated courtrooms of India.

# MARY D'SOUZA SEQUEIRA

## Off the Beaten Track

Little Mary was sad that the girls' convent school she attended had no sports ground. She would spend hours watching her brothers play hockey with other boys on the neighbourhood playground. She soon learnt the game she loved and started playing with the boys after school. In those years, girls' education was no longer uncommon. But it was still not acceptable for girls to participate in outdoor sports that required physical stamina. Mary knew that if she wanted to continue playing hockey, she needed to do better than the boys and get noticed. So she practised hard and outperformed the boys. One of Mary's cousins noticed how fast she was on the field. He enrolled her in a local running competition. This was the first of many races she would win in the days to come.

Mary D'Souza was born in a middle-class Goan family in 1931. Her father, Diogo D'Souza, was a train driver. He was a very hardworking man. Mary's mother, Milagrina D'Souza, spent hours cooking and looking after her children. Mary admired her parents and learnt self-determination from them. Though she enjoyed running and playing hockey, it was not easy for her to choose the career of a sportswoman. Her parents did not encourage her. They did not force her to quit sports, but they never showed any interest in her achievements.

Her father would scold her harshly: 'Better sweep the floors if you need exercise. Do not run around like a mad woman.' She did not have the facilities that professional athletes and players need – not even a proper ground to practise in. Still she did not lose hope. Mary would sneak into the nearby boys' school to practise running on their track.

In 1951, Mary participated in the Asian Games in New Delhi as a runner. She won two medals – silver in the 400-metre relay race and bronze in the 200-metre race. She then went to Madras for the national games in 1952. Little did she know that the authorities were selecting women athletes for the Olympics. When she broke the records in the 200-metre and 100-metre races, she was selected along with three other girls to represent India in the Olympics to be held that year in Helsinki, the capital of Finland. Mary was elated at the news, but she had to overcome many hurdles.

Travelling to Helsinki required a lot of money. Mary could not find sponsors for her trip. She worked as a teacher and earned a paltry sum. The government finally provided some funds, and her friends organized a dance and cards tournament to raise money for her trip. She was happy when she finally boarded the flight. It was her childhood dream to travel by air. The Indian women did not win any games at the Olympics. They did not have professional support and were underprepared. Mary noted that the women's events at the Olympics were both fewer and not as well-attended as the men's events. Though this disappointed her, she made many friends, enjoyed herself and learnt a lot watching the participants from other countries.

Alongside running, Mary continued playing hockey. She participated in the World Cup Hockey Tournament in London in 1953 and the one in Australia in 1956. In those days, playing hockey was difficult for women because the World Hockey Federation did not allow them to wear shorts like the men. Shorts were seen as inappropriate, and women were expected to wear modest clothes. The divided skirts that they had to wear were not conducive for playing hockey.

Shortly after she came back from Helsinki, Mary met a young man named Saluzinho Sequeira at a picnic. She fell in love with him and they got married. Mary started working as a railway sports recruiter. The couple had two children, Marissa and Richard. Marissa too excelled at sports. She played basketball and hockey and participated in track and field events and won medals in all three at the national level. Sadly, Mary did not encourage her daughter to pursue a career in sports. Sports in India was not a well-paying profession for women, she argued. Marissa wrote a book on her mother's life, titled *You Can't Eat Your Fame*.

Though Mary won the Dhyan Chand Award in 2013, she remains largely forgotten. She wants people to know her story. Now in her nineties, she loves watching girls play. She watched the Tokyo Olympics held in 2021 and was elated to see three Indian women win medals. Indian girls have come a long way in sports, but their path was laid out by sportswomen like Mary.

# ARATI SAHA
## Swimming Against the Tide

In Calcutta, there lived a girl who could swim like a mermaid. Her name was Arati. When she was four years old, her paternal uncle, Biswanath Saha, would take her to the River Ganga to bathe. This is where Arati first learnt to swim. Soon, everyone noticed that she could swim tirelessly for hours. One day, Sachin Nag, a famous Indian swimmer, saw Arati swimming in the river. He realized that with proper training she could one day become a champion. He took Arati to the Hatkhola Club of North Calcutta, where she began her formal training. Though Arati came from a lower middle class family where pursuing sports was not easy, she had her father's support. Sports was seen as a man's domain at that time. But, Arati's father wanted his little girl to follow her talent.

In 1945–46, when Arati was only five years old, she won her first swimming medal. In 1949, Arati created a national record in swimming. By the time she was eleven, she had already won twenty-two medals at state-level competitions. In 1952, the twelve-year-old Arati, along with Mary D'Souza Sequeira and two other girls, represented India at the Helsinki Olympics. She was the youngest member of the Indian team.

Arati's next target was to cross the English Channel, the strip of the Atlantic Ocean that flows between northern France and southern England. Mathew Webb, an Englishman, was the first to swim across the Channel in 1875. Since then, crossing the Channel had been a matter of great pride and honour for professional swimmers. It involved long-distance swimming for twenty-one miles. Arati began to train towards this goal. At one point, she would swim continuously for eight hours in a swimming pool in Calcutta. Then, she doubled her time. Arati also swam for long hours in the Ganga. Finally, she was selected by the English Channel Swimming Race Organizers as a contestant in 1959. Her name was recommended to the organizers by Brojen Das, a Pakistani swimmer who had crossed the Channel in 1952. This was a remarkable moment in Arati's career. No Asian woman had swum across the English Channel yet. Arati could create history by becoming the first.

Crossing the Channel was, however, an expensive affair. It involved travel to Europe, regular training and a strict dietary routine. Arati and her family did not have enough money to afford this. Luckily for her, the government stepped in. Bidhan Chandra Roy, the chief minister of West Bengal, and Jawaharlal Nehru, the prime minister of India, approved funding for Arati's training and travel to Europe. In July 1959, Arati reached France. Her race was scheduled on 27 August at 1 a.m. as the condition of the sea would be most favourable at that time, according to experts. She was to swim from Cap Gris-Nez, France, to Sandgate, England. On the night of 27 August, however, something unexpected happened. Arati's pilot boat did not come on time. The boat was to show her the way in the deep sea and rescue her in case of an accident or a health emergency. Arati could not start off without the boat. Fifty-seven other swimmers from all around the world, who were to swim across the English Channel on that day, started at 1 a.m., as per schedule. Their boats had come on time. Arati, however, kept waiting. Her boat finally came at 2 a.m., and Arati began one hour later than the others. After a while, she faced a current from the opposite direction, which made her journey very difficult. Nonetheless, she swam continuously for more than twelve hours. But when she was only a few kilometres away from the English shore, she had to give up owing to the strong water current in the opposite direction. Thus, for no fault of hers, she could not finish the race. Arati, however, decided to stay on in France. After a month, she made another attempt to cross the Channel. Despite a choppy sea, she was successful this time. In sixteen hours and twenty minutes, she had swum more than sixty kilometres to reach Sandgate from France. Thus, after one unsuccessful attempt, Arati became the first Indian and the first Asian woman to cross the English Channel.

For this momentous achievement, Arati received many honours and awards, including the Padma Shri in 1960. To honour Arati's success, the Government of India issued a postage stamp in her name in 1999, five years after the swimmer's death.

Though she did not live a long life, it was a remarkable one. At a time when very few women could think of having a career in sports, Arati's success was an inspiration to many. On Arati's strong, broad shoulders stand the Indian sportswomen of today.

# TUN TUN

## The Queen of Comedy

Uma could not recall how her parents looked. They were killed in a dispute over family land when she was very young. She and her elder brother lived with their uncle. Her brother loved her very much and took good care of her. But, a few years after the death of their parents, he too lost his life.

Uma's uncle was a conservative man who lived in a remote village in Uttar Pradesh. In those days, though girls' education had become very common in cities and towns, most villagers did not send their girls to school. Uma's uncle was no exception – he did not send her to school. Little Uma was made to do household chores. She trained herself to read and write. In her spare time, she roamed around in the fields and climbed trees. Uma was bubbly and witty. But, deep inside her heart, she missed the warmth of a loving home. She loved music and listened to the radio whenever she could. She was a great fan of the famous music director Naushad Ali, who had composed songs for many popular Hindi movies. She wanted to become a singer, but singing was a taboo for girls in the village. Uma nurtured the dream of becoming a playback singer in Naushad's films. Secretly, she sang the songs that she heard on the radio. She hoped and dreamt that one day, All India Radio would air her songs.

When Uma was thirteen, she ran away from her village and took a train to Bombay. After a lot of effort, she managed to approach some music directors in Bombay. She made her debut as a solo playback singer in the 1946 film, *Wamiq Azra*. The title card of the film bore her full name – Uma Devi Khatri.

Uma still nourished her childhood dream of singing in Naushad's films. After spending some time in the film industry, she finally got a chance to meet Naushad. He asked her to sing and was very impressed. He gave her a chance to sing in his film. Thus began a friendship that would yield a series of popular songs that charmed the Indian audience over the next few years. However, Uma's career as a playback singer was short-lived. Playback singing soon became extremely competitive with new entrants like Lata Mangeshkar and Asha Bhosle, who were formally trained and had a greater vocal range. Uma understood that she had lived her dream, albeit a short one.

At this point, her friend Naushad, whom she looked up to as an elder brother, suggested that Uma should try acting in films. Naushad knew that she had an amazing sense of humour and could make people laugh. In 1950, Uma made her debut as a female comedian in Dilip Kumar's film *Babul*. Dilip Kumar gave her the screen name Tun Tun. Everyone loved her performance in the film, and roles started pouring in. Every other hit movie would star her in roles that were written exclusively for her. Over the course of the next four decades, she acted in 198 films. Some of her famous performances were in *Aar Paar* (1954), *Mr & Mrs 55* (1955) and *Namak Halaal* (1982). She worked with all the leading male comedians of her time.

Despite being a popular actor, Tun Tun was sad that there was no variety in the roles that she was cast in. The tragic nature of comedy in popular films was that anyone who was different was seen as odd and funny. Tun Tun was portrayed in these films as an overweight woman who had aspirations, whether to find a loving partner or to seek professional success, and the audience found this funny. Though Tun Tun did not like this portrayal, she consciously used her physical appearance as her strong point to get roles in films. While her female colleagues would be on a diet, she would always carry her tiffin box, full of tasty food, and eat as much as she wanted. When asked about her food habits, she would quip, 'I need to maintain myself, you see!' Tun Tun was not at liberty to lose weight even if she wanted to, since this would risk her not getting roles in films.

Long after Jaddanbai paved the way for women

in the film industry, Tun Tun showed how one could succeed despite stereotypes. With her unabashed humour and lively charm, Tun Tun, the first comedienne of Hindi cinema, challenged many stereotypes at a time when films portrayed women as dainty, coy and self-sacrificing. While her films continue to entertain audiences, her various roles perhaps also tell us that women do not need to look a certain way to have desires and aspirations.

# SUDESHA DEVI

## The Tree-Hugger

*Matu hamru, paani hamru*
 *Hamra hi chhan yi baun bhi!*
(Ours is the earth, Ours is the water
Ours are the fields, forest and fodder!)

This song was composed during the Chipko Movement, one of the most important new social movements aimed at preserving the forests and the environment. In 1973, the government decided to allocate the forest lands in the Himalayan region in Uttar Pradesh (present-day Uttarakhand) to Simon Company. The private company was permitted to fell the trees and use the forests for other commercial purposes. The villages dependent on these forests decided to resist this and protect the area. This was the Chipko Andolan, a non-violent movement led by the tribal women of Uttarakhand. Sudesha Devi was one of the most important leaders of this movement.

As a young girl living with her parents in Chamba, Sudesha met an Englishwoman and Gandhian activist, Sarala Behn. Sarala emphasized the values of sharing, producing and conserving—the basis of women's work in the hills—as the key to environmental sustainability. Sarala's work as a political leader required her to frequently travel and stay away from home. Sudesha was inspired by Sarala's teachings and her life.

Sudesha's village and other villages in the region depended on the forests for their livelihood. Sudesha Devi, along with Gaura Devi, was the key leader in the movement. Sudesha was a young married woman with a daughter when the movement happened. She led a drive to protect the Rampur forests, near her marital village, from the contractors who wanted to cut down the trees. Along with the other young women, she would go into the forest at night to protect the trees. The women would sit around the trees at night, sharing food and singing songs. These acts of friendship kept up their courage against the armed men employed by the contractors to destroy the forest. Guided by their love for the forests, they hugged the trees to prevent the contractors' men from being able to cut them.

Though the movement initially enjoyed support from the men of the village, soon the government came to an agreement with an all-male council. The government could cut the trees in exchange for a cement road and secondary school. While the women too wanted roads and schools in their region, they realized the government was fooling them with these promises. Such development could not be used in exchange for destroying the environment. The women were not ready to give up protecting the trees and refused to be lured into a compromise. Angry at their defiance, the men banned them from meetings, but women like Sudesha continued to be active in their fight to protect the forests and conserve the environment. This meant that Sudesha and her companions also had to go against their own families – their husbands, brothers-in-law and fathers-in-law. For Sudesha and the others, protecting the forest thus became a fight against the men of the family.

The men spent all their money on alcohol and getting drunk. Along with the environmental movement, women like Sudesha protested against these ills. They spoke against the evil practice of alcoholism while taking on company contractors and the local administration. Their voice and protest soon spread like wildfire. The Chipko Movement became so powerful that the government was forced to cancel its contract with the private company. The company retreated without a single tree being felled. It also brought in a fifteen-year ban on the felling of trees in the Himalayan region. Experts believe that these gains of Chipko were central to the framing of the Forest Conservation Act of 1980.

In 1978, Sudesha and her mates became vocal against the government's decision to build a dam on the Tehri river in Garhwal. She clashed with the local police protesting against this dam which would have an environmental fallout in the region. She was jailed for three weeks following this protest. Sudesha Devi and her fearless companions showed the power of women's solidarity and love for forests, and protected future generations from environmental decay.

Sudesha Devi had learnt farming from her father at a young age. This practice of baranaja cropping, or mixed cropping, made the soil so rich that chemical fertilizers were not needed for cropping. In fact, very little water was needed for this. With the government supporting builders and corporations and showing less concern for ecology and the environment, Sudesha Devi looked at other ways in which she could continue her fight to save the environment. She became a part of the Beej Bachao Andolan (Save the Seeds Movement) to distribute native varieties of seeds across the country to prevent plants and crops from extinction and to create more consciousness among the common people of indigenous plants and sustainability.

Today, there is much talk about ecology and environmental protection and the markets are flooded with expensive organic food. But it was a tribal woman called Sudesha Devi who, years ago, showed us how to protect the environment. She protested against its destruction and lived her life in close proximity with nature. Yet, she remains forgotten in history, so much so that even her dates of birth and death remain unrecorded.

# GLOSSARY

BRAHMO: Brahmos are the followers of the Brahmo religion. The Brahmo religion originated in Bengal in the mid-nineteenth century. The followers of this religion believe in one god (monotheism) and superiority of no scripture. Initially it was very popular, particularly among the educated youths. Many converted to the Brahmo religion. Over the years, however, it became more and more similar to Hinduism, and the number of new members reduced. The spread of the Brahmo religion remained limited to Bengal and Bengali-speaking people.

CASTE SYSTEM: The caste system in India traditionally grouped people into four hierarchical caste-groups – the Brahmans, usually priests and scholars; the Kshatriyas, who were rulers and warriors; the Vaishyas or merchants and the Shudras or menial workers, who were regarded as untouchables before the constitution came into being.

COMMUNIST: Communists are the followers of communism, a political ideology that believes in a classless society, where there are no rich and

# GLOSSARY

poor. Communists fight for a society where all wealth and property are owned by the community and not by individuals. The communist ideology was developed by Karl Marx and Friedrich Engels. It has been followed in different ways by different countries across the world. China, Laos and Cuba are among the countries that call themselves communist.

DALIT: Dalit is a Sanskrit word meaning 'downtrodden'. Leaders of untouchable caste groups started calling themselves Dalits in the 1970s. In the Indian Constitution, they are categorized under the 'Scheduled Castes'.

DEVADASI: The literal meaning of the term is server of god. This was a religious practice prevalent in South India, where young girls were given by their parents/guardians to a deity or temple to dedicate the rest of their lives to the worship and service of the deity. They were imagined to be married to the deity and were required to perform various tasks for the upkeep of the temple, including singing and dancing for the deity, and propagating the tradition of classical music and dance. For many years the Devadasi system was seen as a religious practice to please the divine powers, but it was also an exploitative system. These young girls were forced to do many things for the powerful priests and kings under the guise of devotion.

LOK SABHA: The Lok Sabha, also called the House of the People and the Lower House of the Parliament, is the elected house of the Parliament. It consists of 552 members – 530 are elected from the various states, 20 from the union territories and 2 from the Anglo-Indian community. Apart from the last two, all members are elected by the people of the country. The Lok Sabha is the most powerful wing of the Parliament and has the ultimate authority with regard to making or rejecting laws. Unless dissolved earlier, the Lok Sabha operates for five years from its election.

PARLIAMENT: In modern political history, the Parliament is an important part of a democracy. India is a republic, which means that the country is not under the rule of a king, and the state positions are not inherited but elected by the people of the country. The Parliament is the highest legislative body—that is, law-making body—in the country. The country is divided into constituencies and from each constituency a member is elected to be the representative in the Parliament. The Parliament has two houses – an Upper House (Rajya Sabha) and a Lower House (Lok Sabha). The president of India is its head.

PRINCELY STATE: A princely state (also called a Native State or Indian State) was a territory in the Indian subcontinent that was not directly ruled by the British during the colonial period. Such a territory had an Indian ruler who, however, was indirectly under the authority of the British crown through several financial and military treaties and agreements. Important princely states included Kashmir, Junagadh, Hyderabad, various states in present-day Punjab and Rajasthan, Tripura and others.

QUACKERY: This is a kind of dishonest practice, especially in the field of medicine, that is undertaken to mislead people for financial gains.

RAJYA SABHA: The Rajya Sabha, or the Council of States, is the Upper House of the Parliament. It consists of 250 members. 232 members come to the office through indirect elections. The representatives of each state and union territory are elected by the elected members of the legislative assembly of that state and the members of the electoral college of the union territory. The Rajya Sabha is a permanent house and its members remain in office for six years, with one-third of the members retiring every year. Twelve members are nominated by the president from eminent citizens in various fields. The vice president of India is the ex-officio chairman of the Rajya Sabha.

# FAMOUS PERSONALITIES

*Here's a brief introduction to the important personalities, both men and women, who appear throughout the book. These figures hold an irreplaceable place in India's history.*

ANNA CHANDI (1906–1996): Anna Chandi was appointed as the first woman judge of the country. After independence, she became the first woman judge of a high court when she was appointed in the Kerala High Court. She was also the first woman in a commonwealth country to be appointed judge. Apart from her legal practice, Anna Chandi also worked actively for the betterment of women in society. She founded and edited a Malayali journal called *Shrimati*, which became a platform to raise questions against discriminatory practices against women. In 1930, she also ventured into politics by standing for the representative body of the Travancore state, a position which she finally won and held in 1933.

ANNIE BESANT (1847–1933): Annie Besant was a British social reformer and was also part of the Indian Independence movement. In 1889, she became a follower of the Theosophical Society, which emphasized human service, a spiritual evolutionism drawn from both Eastern and Western philosophy. She wrote and lectured on this; some of her work is still considered central to this school. She was international president of the Theosophical Society from 1907 until her death. She was active in educational and humanitarian work in India and became involved in the Indian Independence movement, establishing the Indian Home Rule League in 1916.

B.C. ROY (1882–1962): Bidhan Chandra Roy was a famous medical doctor and freedom fighter. He was a lifelong supporter of the Indian National Congress. In 1948, he became the chief minister of West Bengal, and he remained so till his death. Bidhan Roy is often remembered as the maker of modern West Bengal because he played a key role in building new cities (Durgapur, Kalyani), industries (the dairy industry in Haringhata, iron and steel industry in Durgapur) and institutions (various government colleges, nursing schools) in Bengal. He was both a fellow of the Royal College of Surgeons and a member of the Royal College of Physicians – a rare honour for any doctor.

B.R. AMBEDKAR (1891–1956): Dr Bhimrao Ramji Ambedkar was one of the most important Dalit leaders of India. Ambedkar launched active movements against the practice of untouchability. He organized public movements and marches to open up public drinking water sources for the untouchables. He led a satyagraha in Mahad to win them the right to draw water from the town's main water tank. He also began a struggle for their right to enter Hindu temples. He was the president of the Constituent Assembly responsible for drafting the Constitution of India. He played a major role in making discrimination against untouchability a punishable offence. Dr Ambedkar was the first law minister of India, serving from

# FAMOUS PERSONALITIES

1947 to 1951. Ambedkar campaigned actively for the upliftment of the Dalits throughout his life.

B.T. RANADIVE (1904–1990): Bhalchandra Trimbak Ranadive was a communist politician and an important trade union leader. He was active with the Mumbai textile workers' Girini Kamgar Union and the GIP Railwaymen's Union. He played a major role in 1949 in the general strike supporting the Naval uprising. Ranadive became an important leader of the Communist Party of India's left wing, and in 1964, with the split in the party, he went on to join and lead the Communist Party of India. He was also the first president of the Centre of Indian Trade Union (CITU), the trade union wing of the Communist Party of India (Marxist). After his death the CITU office in Delhi was named after him.

C. RAJAGOPALACHARI (1879–1972): Chakravarti Rajagopalachari was the only Indian governor-general of independent India, serving from 1948 to 1950 on the interim government. For twenty years (1922–42), he served on the Working Committee of the Indian National Congress and was prime minister of his home state of Madras (now Tamil Nadu) from 1937 to 1939 and then from 1952–54. He was the founder of the Swatantra Party, which brought together different groups united against the Congress.

JAWAHARLAL NEHRU (1889–1964): Jawaharlal Nehru was a freedom fighter and the first prime minister of independent India. As prime minister, he focussed on building new cities, constructing dams on important rivers and establishing big industries in various parts of India. He is also known for building various institutes for scientific research. Nehru was a great writer and wrote about the history of India and that of the world. He disliked violence in the name of religion, and during his rule, he worked hard to bring peace and harmony between the Hindus and Muslims of India.

JYOTIRAO PHULE (1827–1890): Jyotirao Phule, also known as Mahatma Jyotiba Phule, was a social reformer and thinker in nineteenth-century India. He played a leading role in fighting various caste restrictions in India. He criticized the domination of the Brahmins and upheld the cause of the lower castes. He was also a pioneer of women's education in India. Along with his wife Savitribai Phule, he fought for girls' education throughout his life, opening many schools for them.

M.K. GANDHI (1869–1948): Mohandas Karamchand Gandhi was arguably the greatest leader of the Indian national movement. He was a lawyer, social activist and politician, instrumental in leading three of the biggest national movements against the British – the Non Cooperation Movement, Civil Disobedience Movement and Quit India Movement. Gandhi's doctrine of non-violence is renowned all over the world. He is considered to be one of the most important international personalities.

RABINDRANATH TAGORE (1861–1941): A poet, author, music composer, playwright, educationist and social reformer, Rabindranath Tagore was born in a famous family in Bengal. He was awarded the Nobel Prize in Literature for his collection of poems *Gitanjali* in 1913. Recognizing his talent, the King of England awarded him knighthood. Tagore renounced the title because he was upset about the killing of hundreds of Indian civilians by the British Police in the infamous Jallianwala Bagh massacre. Tagore composed about 2000 songs, two of which were chosen as the national anthems of India and Bangladesh. In his writings, Tagore was vocal about the importance of India's freedom struggle. However, his ideas were often unique and unconventional. This led to many interesting debates between him and other great thinkers of his time.

S.A. DANGE (1899–1991): Shripad Amrit Dange, along with Ranadive, was an important leader of the trade union movement, for which he was imprisoned by the colonial government for sixteen years. In 1925 he

## FAMOUS PERSONALITIES

became the founding member of the Communist Party of India. He was the party chairman in 1962. He was elected as a member of the British Legislative Assembly from 1946 to 1951, and as a member of the second and fourth Lok Sabhas from the Bombay City Central constituency. He is credited with successfully spearheading the formation of the state of Maharashtra in 1960.

SUBHAS CHANDRA BOSE (1897–1945): Subhas Chandra Bose was a leading figure in India's freedom struggle. Bose was a brilliant student, who joined the Indian National Congress under the leadership of Gandhi. However, his opinion often differed from the Congress Party's, and finally, he formed his own party – the All India Forward Bloc. He was very popular among the people of India because of his radical views on the importance of revolutionary struggle. He travelled to many countries, including the Soviet Union, Germany and Japan to gain global support for India's freedom struggle. Bose died in a tragic plane crash in 1945. Many of his followers refused to believe that he died in this accident and waited for his return.

# LIST OF SOURCES

*Here is a list of sources that you can refer to should you wish to obtain more information about some of the women discussed in the book, their lives and their many achievements. Do note that there is very little information available in print or digital literature about the finer details relating to the lives of these women who, despite their greatness, remain relatively unknown and undocumented. This book is an effort at filling this gap.*

A. Lalitha
1. Tanvi Patel, 'Married at 15, Widowed at 18: How a Single Mom Became India's 1st Woman Engineer!', *The Better India*, 8 June 2019, Available at: https://www.thebetterindia.com/185532/india-first-woman-engineer-a-lalitha-inspiring-history/.

Bhikaji Cama
1. Sanchari Pal, 'Remembering Madam Bhikaji Cama, the Brave Lady to First Hoist India's Flag on Foreign Soil', *The Better India*, 24 September 2016, Available at: https://www.thebetterindia.com/69290/madam-bhikaji-cama-flag-stuttgart-india/.

Bibha Chowdhuri
1. Amitabha Bhattacharya, 'The Woman Who Could Have Won a Nobel', *The Telegraph*, 25 November 2018, Available at https://www.telegraphindia.com/science-tech/the-woman-who-could-have-won-a-nobel/cid/1676488.
2. Suprakash Roy and Rajinder Singh, 'Historical Note: Bibha Chowdhuri – Her Cosmic Ray Studies in Manchester', *Indian Journal of History of Science,* Vol. 53 Iss. 3, 2018.
3. Suprakash Roy and Rajinder Singh, *A Jewel Unearthed: Bibha Chowdhuri, The Story of an Indian Scientist*, Shaker Verlag, 2018.

Chandraprabha Saikaiani
1. Divya Sethu, 'Meet the Assam Freedom Fighter Who Dared Be a Single Mother & Pioneered Women's Rights', *The Better India*, 23 March 2021, Available at: https://www.thebetterindia.com/251602/chandraprabha-saikiani-assam-woman-freedom-fighter-womens-education-single-mother-india-history-div200/.
2. Avanti Balachander, 'Chandraprabha Saikiani: Breaking Barriers in Women's Education', *Feminism in India*, 16 March 2018, Available at: https://feminisminindia.com/2018/03/16/chandraprabha-saikiani-reforming-education/.

Mary D'Souza
1. G Viswanath, 'Mary D' Souza, India's Track and Field Trailblazer', *Sportstar*, 10 July 2021, Available at: https://sportstar.thehindu.com/athletics/mary-d-souza-indias-track-and-field-trailblazer-first-female-olympian-1952-helsinki-olympics-interview/article35247238.ece.

Swarnakumari Devi
1. Sudhir Chandra, *The Oppressive Present: Literature and Social Consciousness in Colonial India*, Oxford University Press, 1994, p. 112.
2. Teresa Hubel, 'A Mutiny of Silence: Swarnakumari Devi's Sati', *ARIEL*, Vol. 41 Iss. 3–4, 2010, p. 167–190, Available at: http://works.bepress.com/teresa_hubel/2/.
3. Chitra Deb, *Thakurbarir Andarmahal*, Ananda Publishers Pvt Ltd, 2014.
4. Abhijit Sen and Abhijit Bhattacharya, Introduction, *Swarnakumari Devir Sankalito Prabandha*, Bikalpa Prakashani, 1998.

ANWESHA SENGUPTA teaches history at the Institute of Development Studies, Kolkata. She has a PhD in history from Jawaharlal Nehru University.

SUPURNA BANERJEE is a feminist sociologist with a PhD in Sociology from the University of Edinburgh. She works at the Institute of Development Studies, Kolkata.

SIMANTINI MUKHOPADHYAY is a development economist with a PhD in Economics from the University of Calcutta. She works at the Institute of Development Studies, Kolkata.

MISTUNEE CHOWDHURY is a Delhi-based freelance illustrator, animator, painter and sculpture artist. Her work has been featured in several books, including those from the National Book Trust, Hachette, HarperCollins Publishers, Penguin Random House and Scholastic.

## ALSO IN THE TIMELESS BIOGRAPHIES SERIES

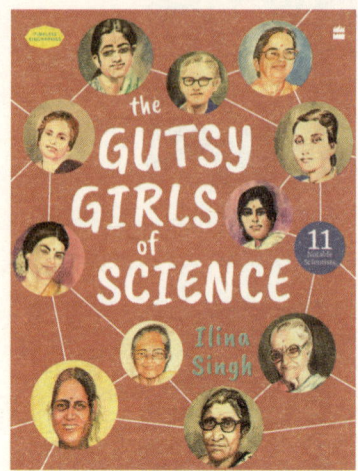

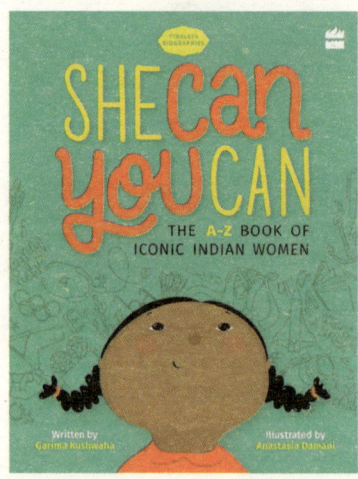